STRESEMANN

GUSTAV STRESEMANN

A PHOTOGRAPH TAKEN AT KARLSBAD IN 1928

STRESEMANN

BY

RUDOLF OLDEN

TRANSLATED BY

R. T. CLARK

WITH THIRTEEN ILLUSTRATIONS

METHUEN & CO. LTD.
36 ESSEX STREET W.C.
LONDON

First Published in 1930

PRINTED IN GREAT BRITAIN

CONTENTS

LIST OF ILLUSTRATIONS

* *Photos: B. A. Balassa, Berlin*
† *Photos: A.B.C. Aktuelle Bilder Centrale, Berlin*

STRESEMANN

'ONLY THE MAN WHO CAN CHANGE
REMAINS KIN TO ME.'

—NIETZSCHE

STRESEMANN

CHAPTER I

THE TINY ROOM

BISMARCK grew up on his father's estates and in the court society of the capital, threw up the career of government official to return to the independent life of a country gentleman and entered political life as a 'wilde Junker'. Caprivi, 'the man without ear or stalk', was an officer in the army, that sphere of unlimited possibilities, and rose to high rank before, at the bidding of his supreme war lord, he became the political leader of the nation. Hohenlohe, a South German princeling, allied to the Royal House of England, at home everywhere in high society, married to a half-Russian princess, surveyed the world with the interested indifference of a citizen of the world and a *grand seigneur*. Bülow's father was a diplomatist; his mother was a member of one of Hamburg's great patrician families; early in life he gained knowledge of countries, men, and tongues; his wife, Princess Maria of the House of Camporeale, had the strongest influence on his life. The Bethmanns, originally *bourgeois* of Goslar, were famous Frankfurt bankers whose daughter married their confidential clerk Hollweg; the Bethmann-Hollwegs became Prussian citizens, landed gentry of Hohenfinow in the Mark, professors, government officials, theologians ; Theobald the Chancellor had risen high in the feudal administration. Michaelis — that sorry episode — belonged to the higher ranks of officialdom and to the worthy of the land.

Bismarck served in the Jägers, and at his own choice passed into memory as a cavalry general, complete with sabre, helmet, and top-boots. Caprivi was a general of infantry ; Bülow was a hussar of the Rhine. Bethmann-Hollweg, who had no inclinations to militarism, became a dragoon of the Guard and reached the rank of major-general. Michaelis, whose desire for military promotion ended by becoming a jest, was a major when he was raised to the highest office of the State and declared that ' never would he let the rudder slip from his hands '. Of all the chancellors of the Hohenzollern Empire only the aristocrat Hohenlohe and the Catholic Hertling wore civilian dress, and both were old men when they came to power. Stresemann once said that the German people could neither understand nor admit that a civilian could be Minister of War. A contrary proposition is equally true : the German people under the Hohenzollern rule seems never to have been able to endure that its Chancellor, the leader of Parliament and the conductor of foreign affairs, should be a civilian, even if Wilhelm II did call him in scorn ' the civil Chancellor '. When his nomination appeared in the *Official Gazette*, there appeared simultaneously in the *Militärwochenblatt* the news of his promotion and assumption of a uniform. Naked, he was clothed ; and when he appeared before the representatives of the people with a message from his Imperial master, spurs jingled on his boots. There were considerations too of a sentimental order ; the Minister of War or the Chief of the General Staff was higher in rank, and in a sense was quite recognizably his superior officer.

The Chancellors were princes, counts, nobles, landed gentry, members of the court, men of property who had passed their youth in the schools and colleges of the aristocracy. Then came sons of the mighty, the catholic, 'universal' Church, straitly allied to the Lord of all Christendom. Later still they were Social Democrats, men who had a broad outlook of another type, who early had sworn allegiance to the international of socialism, of trade unions and political parties, who had seen foreign countries, who, area secretaries and provincial editors, felt themselves to be members of a world-wide, world-conquering organization and leaders of the international working class. There were no wide horizons where Stresemann was born.

No. 66 Kopenicker Strasse, the house in which he was born on May 19, 1878, and grew up, still stands there to-day, just as it was then, insignificant, narrow, three-storied. Others a story higher and decked out with all the meretricious ornamentalism of the end of the century, have been built beside it and opposite it. But, if one can for a moment forget the tram-lines and the taxicabs, the street has really not changed much in fifty years. Even at that time, before there were any of the great boulevards of the west end, it was only a tiny street ; it always lay in a lower middle-class quarter, a little to the south of and away from the business centre of Berlin. The tiny shop on the ground floor is still there, but it has become still tinier. Once there were steps outside it ; now, because the traffic has grown, the steps are inside. That is the only change in fifty years. In this shop Stresemann *père* conducted what was then called a *boutique*—a beer-shop. To-day an innkeeper who sells the local beer is still called a '*Budiker*'; but the trade was different fifty years ago. Then it had other bases, which capitalism and the big breweries have destroyed. The economics student Gustav Stresemann devoted his thesis for his doctor's degree to that change which he had experienced in his own life and whose consequences had singularly affected it. This was the epoch of the 'white beer', and just as important as the providing of this specifically Berlin drink was the care in its handling and bottling. In the elder Stresemann's cellar there were always three to four men at this important task. He was famed for the pains he took with his excellent beer. Like champagne, white beer ferments in the bottle a second time. When it is poured into the great big-bellied goblets, from which it should be drunk, it foams up sparkling without the aid of soda-water. That is its special quality, and differentiates it from the Bavarian beer by which it was conquered.

The elder Stresemann's chief business was not sale in the house, but delivery to the works in the neighbourhood. At that time total abstinence or a temperance movement was as little thought of by the Berlin workers as the eight-hour day. At the second breakfast and at the midday meal, and also in many cases at the evening meal, a bottle of beer was an invariable companion. Milk was a drink for children ; a grown man would have found distinctly amusing the suggestion that it would quench his thirst. So the elder Stresemann always delivered daily hundreds of bottles of beer to the workers in the neighbouring State printing-works. There was also established an interesting credit system. The bottler at the beginning of the week gave a young agent coupons, which in the course of the week the agent gave to the workers and for which they procured beer, herring, raw meat, and other components of a worker's meal. On Saturday, which was pay day, the agent collected the sums represented by the coupons issued and settled his account there and then, minus ten per cent commission. This system brought the bottler and the consumer into closer relationship. On Sunday the worker did not need to trouble about his provender for the next week: the innkeeper could reckon on a definite number of customers. Thus he was in a biggish way of business; he was a beer-retailer. About 1900, at a time before the word became fashionable, there was a good deal of rationalization, and the big breweries put an end to the practice. They got rid of the middlemen by setting up canteens of their own in the factories, and a whole section of the middle class disappeared from the economic life of the nation. But until that time there was good money in such business, especially when it was conducted so skilfully and so energetically as Stresemann's parents conducted it. As early as six o'clock one could have seen Stresemann senior, a big, upstanding figure of a man, his waning locks carefully draped over the bald patches, standing outside his house feeding the pigeons which the noise and roar of a cosmopolitan capital had not yet driven away. From that early hour until late in the evening Stresemann's mother stood behind the counter and served her customers. When his trade was ruined by the extension of capitalist methods, the elder Stresemann was not merely owner of the house in which he had laid the foundations of a successful business, but was the landlord of several other tenement buildings. He was well able to provide for his children or for children-in-law, and nothing stood in the way of his opening the higher education to his youngest son, who had shown special aptitude for it.

The large Stresemann family lived on the first floor of that narrow-fronted house which was No. 66 Kopenicker Strasse. There were the five long, narrow bedrooms and the best room ; the parlour was on the ground floor. The common room adjoined the shop, and behind the former was the parlour, with its window overlooking the yard, and near at hand if ever either father or mother had a free moment. Here, over his homework, when school was done, sat the young Gustav. Here he wrote his essays, here he wrote his first poetry, here, where innumerable books were piled one on top of the other, he dreamed boyish dreams of fame.

It was in the years around 1890 that the youngest Stresemann received his most durable impressions. Berlin was very much smaller then than it is to-day, but even then it was a great city and its boundaries were more distant than they are nowadays. No motor-buses, no electric railways hurried folk to woods and lakes. There were no scouts, no ramblers, seeking open spaces with their knapsacks and their guitars. Those who settled down amid those tall houses stayed there. What physical training there

BIRTHPLACE
NO. 66 KÖPENICKER STRASSE,
BERLIN

STRESEMANN AS CORPS STUDENT

STRESEMANN AS A SCHOOLBOY

HERR AND FRAU STRESEMANN
AT THE TIME OF THEIR MARRIAGE

was, was but a poor imitation of what one got in the army; there were no football clubs, no rowing clubs, no cycling associations for the sons of the middle class.

Berlin and Berlin life were stale and prosy to a degree that it is almost impossible to conceive to-day, and nowhere could it be prosier than in Kopenicker Strasse, among the works and factories, small business houses, shops and working-class tenements. Yet in the long room looking out into the yard, to which the boy returned when school was over, there dwelled romance. Indeed, the drabber the surroundings, the more colourful the thoughts that were thought among them. The sea, colonies, the greatness of the nation, a free people on a free soil, the Empire, the great ones of the earth—Frederick, Napoleon, Goethe—these filled his soul.

It was a cynical time, this German age of get-rich-quickery. Socialism was the affair of the workers; for the ruling class it was simply an opportunity to issue police prohibitions, sentences of imprisonment, and sentences of expulsion; but it was in no way the affair of the middle-class inhabitants of the Kopenicker Strasse. Cynical was the rude determination with which the Junker class strove to rule this new aspiring Germany in the old manner; cynical was the obtrusive snobbery of the middle class, whereby it sought to assimilate itself to the Junkers; cynical the cold-blooded careerism of the gilded youth; cynical the enthusiasm for brute force, for victory and the army; cynical the contempt for literature and art. But that cynicism never reached the long room behind the shop. Father and grandfather had only been able to attend the primary school, and his brothers and sisters got no farther. Only to the Benjamin of the family was the way opened to higher things. Here at least education and culture were something where they were like rain on dry soil, which will be greedily absorbed. The bitterness at the vicious and dangerous indifference of the ruling class which drove the new generation of writers to denial of the State as well as of the conventional standards of beauty had no place here; naturalism had no appeal. Where all around was hateful, the beauty of hatefulness naturally was not appreciated. There were no decadents here; hearts were flung wide open to the splendour of the older literature and to that wonder of history which is at the same time a promise. There was no arrogance, no revolutionaryism; there was belief, acceptance. The house which the family lived in was a prosy place, but its prosiness was a sound foundation on which to build, and in it there was that romance which is in the life of every great man to claim devotion. Prose and romance—these are two worlds, and then, as even later, Stresemann moved in both. And to all this there was added the will to greatness, the will to power.

These three elements were not usually found in Stresemann's contemporaries. His generation was not capable of great feeling; it was cold; not realist, but fantastic; clear in its preferences, but not resolved to conquer power. Fate had thrown riches and great possibilities into its lap. The Empire, of which an unforeseen development had made a present to the German *bourgeoisie*, was not achieved by the nation; it was created by one man—by

Bismarck—who was in Germany an isolated phenomenon. After him it seemed as if the growing might of Germany had exhausted itself in the birth of this one superman.

Bismarck's own verdict on the Prussians which he delivered towards the end of his life is cruel, even shattering. He declared that his land could produce competent officers up to the rank of regimental commanders, but never anything better. And he had lived and worked with the old Prussian type of loyal and devoted officers and officials; under the glare of Kaiserism that type disappeared.

Equally that solidity which had distinguished the contemporaries of Wilhelm I was destroyed by display, intrigue, and tuft-hunting. The good qualities of the upper classes of the nation degenerated, as they do under the influence of strong drink. Shallowness and presumption took their place, and an intolerable conceit ascribed all the success, which a happy combination of circumstances had produced, to the brilliance of native qualities. This was the epoch when Germany drew down upon herself the hate of the whole world. Yet that hate, expressed far too violently to be ignored, served but to heighten the conceit of a blinded generation. Not only did Albion, proverbially the 'envious' nation, hate, but all the other nations hated Germany because she surpassed them. The spirit of Stein and Hardenberg, of Scharnhorst and Gneisenau, had created those reserves of national strength out of which the genius of Bismarck had created the Empire; now that spirit had departed. It survived no more than did the honesty of Wilhelm I and his generation. What remained was a gigantic military power established in the middle of Europe, a fortunate combination of iron and coal, a working class which is the most industrious in the world, and the milliards of the war-indemnity which acted as a fierce stimulant to the worst instincts of acquisitiveness. The worthy elements of the nobility withdrew, shocked and embittered, from a court where flunkeys and upstarts had free rein. The intellectuals, the artists, fled from the Empire and, if they could, from the Empire's capital; they became revolutionaries hostile to the State and sought a new home among the workers. The great industrialists, in whom the old traditions still lived, turned away with disgust from the gilt and tinsel of the new régime. Clear-sighted men, who recognized the disease from which the nation was suffering, passed into hopeless opposition; there was nothing else for them to do but make their purely negative protest.

Since it practically did not exist, the joy of responsibility became a mere phrase to the new generation. Actually any use or exercise of power was for them a mere derivation from a higher class. Bismarck had accustomed people to such a state of things, and had brought them up to believe that a stronger looked after them. When the great man, the stronger, had passed, people transferred this confidence in an inexhaustible source of strength to his successor—Wilhelm II. Only men dazzled and intoxicated by the vision of the brilliance of the age could have permitted the founder of the Empire to be dismissed without making a protest. Ambition took the place of sober calculation. The pleasing fantasy gained the day that the young overlord would give the same—nay, better—leadership than the tried statesman whom he had brutally kicked from power. There was no consciousness that every citizen had responsibility to the State and the nation.

A friend, who used to accompany the sixteen-year-old Gustav to the dancing-classes which an old ballet-trainer held in a house behind the Holzmarktstrasse, tells us that the young folk there were all children of the east end. Their fathers were artisans, shopkeepers, and small officials. Money for most of them was scarce, very scarce, and only acquired by hours of extra work. Stresemann of the secondary school, the son of a beer merchant in a big way, was considered to be prosperous. Of Stresemann himself he says: 'Stresemann wore a long overcoat. His shoulders stooped slightly and his head inclined forwards. His hair was fair and thick. He was more serious than the rest of us, even a little melancholy'—his much-loved mother had died just a little time before this—'and staider than we older ones. Also he was shyer.'

That shyness was something deeper than mere bashfulness. The head of the Andreas College, which he attended, told him that he would never be a success unless he conquered this weakness. In the room behind the tap-room among the many books, the soul was not free and at ease in the world. Thirty years later Stresemann told how he had struggled under 'pure study—learning'. In his commemoration of Rathenau he wrote, remembering his own youth, 'Accustomed to wealth and to wide horizons he belonged to those who like the members of the old nobility had naturally an assurance which others must painfully acquire.' But the tiny room was very convenient for a student.

Freedom of expression, freedom of thought came to him there, and here the youth gave knowledge sure foundations.

The young Stresemann was so little in sympathy with the average youth of the day that he never recognized its chief characteristics. Its indifferent atheism was as foreign to him as its sham elegance or its self-seeking conceit. Before his leaving certificate examination a secondary schoolboy writes a *curriculum vitae*. How earnest and introspective he was may be seen from his composition :

> ' My first impulse to thinking about religion came when I was preparing for confirmation under the present General Superintendent, then Court Chaplain, Faber. There were only a few of us in the confirmation class, so that Chaplain Faber was able to devote himself to us and influence us individually. This was the easier because he scarcely ever accepted candidates who did not come from the secondary schools, a practice which I could not approve although I have to thank it for a good deal of the inspiration I received. Although often I was not able to follow that highly cultured man in his intellectual flight, yet I owe to his teaching a deep influence on my mind and soul.'

With the same melancholic introspection he proceeded to set down the fundamentals of his religious belief. They are an extract from a much more comprehensive confession of faith :

> ' I believe in God as the creator of the world. I believe in Jesus Christ as the Son of God, since

the Divine nature revealed itself in him in the purest and most sublime form. His words and teachings appear to me the noblest and most exalted revelation of the Divine will, and consequently I regard them as the basis of Christianity. If there is a Last Judgement, then I believe that our whole life, in so far as it was a fulfilment or a failure to fulfil the Divine will, will be the standard by which we shall be judged, and not the actual membership of this or that religious body, or our adherence to this or that dogma. Consequently I believe that it is absolutely essential that there should be the most complete tolerance in all matters of faith.'

The liberal bases, approved a generation later, when the Republic planned its education law, are all there in that youthful confession. Much that was revealed in the politician was already in the student. In the last years of his school life what interested him especially were his classes in religious instruction, literature, and history. These may be described as the studies of the politician. They certainly were the studies of the young Stresemann.

He never was completely at home in economics, to which he turned since that study opened to him the door to a career. Even in the matter of industrial organization, or in the later problems of inflation and of reparations to which he had to devote himself, he at once sensed and understood their political aspect.

It was the same with literature, which filled his note-books in his first term at college and to which he returned so often. The romances of Friedrich

Spielhagen, which as a boy he devoured, contained, besides banal love stories, descriptions of social life. When the eighteen-year-old student spoke on poetry at the 'Scientific Society', what was his theme? The revolutionary poetry of the first half of the century: Herwegh, Freiligrath, Dingelstadt, Grün, and Gilm—all political poets. With aestheticism his love of literature had no connexion. His own verses were almost always what Goethe calls occasional poetry; he paid attention to meaning, to significance rather than to form, which he simply adopted without giving the choice much thought. When as deputy and Minister he spoke of Goethe, he seeks to vindicate his hero from the reproach of having had no sympathy with the War of Independence, or seeks to show that the great German refused to bow to the great Emperor.

His never-failing memory retained all that he read with real love, and in many speeches he finds that the words of much-loved poets alone can express his feelings. In his quotations he showed more than the virtuosity that distinguished his predecessor, Bülow; he shows sensitiveness, warmth, appreciation. Yet an aesthete among his colleagues said later that he felt a shiver down the spine every time the Minister quoted Goethe.

In art Stresemann was a politician; in politics he showed that he was a gifted artist. When he was only nineteen in that 'Scientific Society' of students and apprentices to commerce he pulled to pieces the Erfurt Programme of the Social Democrats and professed a social Liberalism. In debate he was so ready, so brilliant, that the friend of his youth who tells us about it coins the fine phrase, 'He bubbled over with politics.' A diplomatist who was present with him at many conferences thirty years after was so impressed by the same qualities that he said, ' He was brimful of politics ' and ' in debate he was winged with music '. Here is Stresemann's talent masterfully summarized. The Muses forbade him to enter their kingdom, but they accompanied him when he entered his own of politics.

What the young Berliner was in his debating society so the politician remained at Locarno, at Geneva, in The Hague. Stresemann, one of the first professional politicians in Germany, was a politician born. Ability of the highest order revealed itself and could only be expressed musically, sensuously, artistically. The German language has no word for the quality which the French call *flair*—the sense of the trail, the unerring faculty of discerning the strength and weakness of the opponent, and so where one can concede, where one must remain inflexible, the eye of the hunter, the nose of the hunting hound for the twists and turns of the adversary at the green tables, qualities which no knowledge, no intellectual ability can supply but are inborn, and which are nowhere rarer than in our land ; these were Stresemann's. We saw him in his schoolboy days, melancholic, *gauche*, shy. That was at the dancing-class. Now he looks others in the face, attacks them boldly, sword in hand, checkmates them, yet remains their friend. He has found his element.

Stresemann's romantic nature delighted in the wearing of the coloured cap and the scarf of the students' corps. Membership of a corps which was closely connected with the upper classes depended far less on the personality of the student than on the position and the bank balance of his father. Entry into a corps was then, far more than it is to-day, a matter of ' connexions '. The new student fresh from school entered the corps with which he already had ' connexions ', and he entered it to get more ' connexions ' through it—one good turn always deserving another. This does not merely hold true of the corps, say, of Bonn, Heidelberg, or Göttingen, in which only the sons of high society were to be found. Other corps too had their clique of old members who never severed their connexion with the corps, and were delighted to lend a helping hand to young members when they passed from the university to Philistia, to a career. This Philistia, this world outside so reviled in students' songs, was precisely what the corps members had their eyes on when they displayed such enthusiasm for the rattle of beer-mugs. It was a sign of that cynical and fantastically-conceived epoch, that the laced coats which German students had long ago adopted out of sympathy with the revolutionaries of Poland now covered nothing but sheer careerism, a desire for titles, for orders, for salaries.

The student Stresemann entered a newly-founded corps. There was no special recommendation required for membership. The members came for the most part, like Stresemann, from the lower middle class. The idea of the founders was to revive the old ideal of the corps which had gone down in defeat before the noise and rattle of the Hohenzollern Empire. It was a hopeless venture. The strength of the old corps was now too great, too firmly rooted on real and realist bases for a young corps to shake them. Never was such a revolution possible. Those to whom false glamour did not appeal went to the free corps, which, without using compulsion, kept together the students not eligible for the old corps. But to the young man from the tiny room behind the shop the brightness of the colours was attractive. And as for all that he sought earnestness and reality, also as he had social sensitiveness and the feeling of national unity, and even appreciation of the brilliance of the new Empire, he joined the Reform Union, which sought in the Germany of black, red, and white to revive the black, red, and gold ideals of the old corps. He himself, although not in the least a revolutionary, once laid a wreath in the name of his fellows and in company with labour men and democrats on the graves of the dead of March 1848; his own grandfather had been one of the fighters for freedom in that year. The resolution of his corps which laid this duty upon him had been drawn up by himself. At a time when nothing was heard but panegyric of the Empire, the army, the fleet, this commemoration of the lost democratic revolution which he brought about was unique. He had the courage once again to choose an individual path away from those of the crowd. Yet he did not admire the new Empire any the less. Much later the romantic idea came to him of the possibility in a time of political crisis to unite the two flags and the two ideals.

Student life did not take the young Stresemann very far from his home in the Kopenicker Strasse. He went on living in Berlin, and only for six months went to Leipzig. In the great industrial city students counted for little. That withdrawal from life which is possible in a small university, where

2

students' corps and unions are as powerful as orders in which their own customs rule, in which there may even be spoken a dialect, a jargon, that is incomprehensible to outsiders, that self-conceit which made the old corps so spiritually barren could not exist there. If it did, in spite of everything, it was merely grotesque. In the Reform Unions the political ideas of the time were reflected. Stresemann, even in his second term the leader of his comrades, wrote in their magazine a medley of articles and essays on religious, philosophic, and political questions.

Later he set down what his political convictions were in those days. Friedrich Naumann, pastor and politician, founder of National Socialism, editor of a periodical called *Help*, which was always in need of it, had failed to found a party which would fill Germany with a new life of virtue and spirituality. The people refused to follow him, and later he resigned himself to joining the Liberals in order to have some political influence. But as a National Socialist he had powerfully impressed the young. When he died in the summer of 1919 the opposition between the leaders of the People's Party and of the Democrats was at its height; the bitterness of the separation from friends who had passed to other parties was still fresh; the miscarriage of the attempt to unite Liberalism was a recent and painful memory. But the loss of this honoured friend impelled Stresemann to a eulogy which no party colleague could have made warmer or more sincere. The impressions of youth returned, that youth in which the romance of the sword and the coloured cap was joined to the romance of a monarchical socialism.

Stresemann bewailed the fact that a leader of youth should have mixed in the degrading business of parliamentarianism and wrote:

> 'Naumann was and will remain the great spiritual inspirer and awakener, especially by his activities at the beginning of the century. How we young students cheered him in his war against the narrowness and the corruption of German party politics. We could not join the Social Democrats. Everything in us called out against their negation of nationalism, and their Marxist brand of socialism. Liberalism had lost its power to appeal; it had become mere Manchesterism with Eugen Richter, and with the National Liberals a mere battle-field for conflicting tendencies. To join Stocker was impossible for the Liberal thinker because of his orthodoxy and the consequent Christian Socialist campaign in Berlin. Then came Friedrich Naumann who in this time of ferment, with its search for new ideas, threw out the ideal of the alliance of the Imperial Throne with German Labour.'

But Naumann, who had let himself be elected to the Reichstag, 'the most wearisome place of oratory in the world', with its 'prosaic, dull atmosphere of the commonplace', and now 'deferred to the debating-merchants who sought safety in the lobbies when debate was over, where they could give free rein to a cynicism that cheapened everything', although he spoke over the heads of the three hundred and ninety-seven gentlemen of Parliament to the people and over the heads of the people to humanity. But he made 'no great speeches now for the German army, for the German colonies, for the German element abroad '. When Stresemann thanks the dead leader ' for all that he gave us of social conscience in the epoch of the triumph of Manchesterism ', he speaks of himself, of his own youth. The ideas of 1848 were again alive in him ; they were intermingled with much later ideas of social emancipation. In the meantime he tramped for long the road of commonplace activity, became secretary of a union of industrialists, left ' the army of officers without soldiers ', as he called the National Socialist League, joined the National Liberals, became deputy and then leader of the party. At Naumann's grave the world of romance returned, that world which he had seen from the tiny room behind the bar—colonies, the fleet, the Empire, the happiness of the worker, brilliance and nobility, greatness and justice. He travelled back a long road, a road that had led to success but was filled with bitterness. He himself had become a professional parliamentarian, a member of the body of which he spoke so harshly, he acquired his habits, he was the Benjamin of the Reichstag and for long played on that difficult instrument with all the skill of a virtuoso. But in imagination this ex-member of the Reform Union was sitting once again at the feet of Friedrich Naumann. ' Every man who concerns himself with the problem of the present and the future gives his best at those moments when he is free from the fetters of a party outlook.' This idea occurs again in the preface he wrote for a German edition of the speeches of Aristide Briand : ' In Parliament the party system fetters the free functioning of opinion.'

There is another thing that is full of significance in this funeral oration. If the battle-line loses coherence and the troops are scattered, some simply stay where they are, others march on in a solid mass, or one by one. Some are in front, some in rear, and, although all of them keep direction, yet they cannot help but think that they seek different objectives, and one thinks the other a traitor. Once upon a time Friedrich Naumann had jeered at the young Stresemann who had gone into business and become a National Liberal. In the funeral oration Stresemann reproached the dead leader for abandoning the Empire. He said he had never understood why ' the man who as none other had pleaded for the union of the democracy and the Empire had declared in his first speech to the National Assembly that eternal farewell must be taken of the Empire '.

Early convictions do not signify much to a politician. It is more important for him to judge rightly in the actual moment of decision. It is always useless for him simply to be able to say that he foresaw or foretold an event, if his knowledge and his prophecy were barren of result. The actions of the politician, just like those of an ordinary mortal, are determined by feeling rather than by intellectual conviction ; their reasons have to be sought rather in the unconscious than the conscious. His intelligence finds arguments for his actions : his actions do not arise from reflection. Politics is an art not a science. That man is a statesman who at the right time acquires the conviction of the rightness of what he is going to do.

When the King of Prussia, who possessed the presidency of the Bundesrat and also the Imperial

title, was finding his support in the army, the great landowning class, and the aristocratic bureaucracy, Naumann was preaching the People's Empire. His influence remained confined to the hordes of students; he reached the Emperor no more than he convinced the workers. With the army fell kingdom and Empire together. The Social Democrat Scheidemann had already said that a monarchy of the English type was preferable in his opinion for Germany to a money-bag republic like the French —so he called to life the German Republic. He did, in spite of his own arguments, what the hour commanded. Stresemann adopted the slogan, the People's Empire, when he stood in opposition to the Republican majority. Then, as before, it appealed to his sense of romance. During the war such a conception had had no influence on events; now it was effective, it served to rally the middle class, whose representative he was. The realization that the Empire had become impossible because its natural bases had disappeared only came to him later than to Naumann, who had understood more quickly the consequences of what was happening. But if the battle-line loses coherence and the individuals compose it march individually to their objective, it is not he who gets there first who is the most important person on the field, but he who rallies the dispersed troops. The man who creates a rallying-point lives in history as a statesman.

The People's Empire, a phrase from Naumann's vocabulary, a phrase out of his own romantic youth, was for Stresemann's later policy only a significant expression, an idea which might serve as a basis for agitation. But in his attitude to the social question

Naumann's influence was permanent. Just as when he was an industrial organizer, Stresemann never was an extremist, so against violent opposition he always upheld the workers' right to share in responsibility and steadily demanded and furthered the participation of the Social Democrats in the government.

Stresemann had intended to obtain his doctor's degree with a comprehensive work of theory; actually he got it for a short thesis on the development of the bottled-beer industry. His theme was one that affected him very closely. He studied scientifically what he himself had actually experienced. His theme was his father's fate, the fate of the independent lower middle class of Berlin, which was ruined by the pressure of capitalist development. It lost position after position and was violently expelled from the way of life which it had so long enjoyed. Marbled bank-buildings and workers' tenements, these remained; the beer-shops with the tiny room in which Stresemann had grown up disappeared. With the middle class, Dr. Stresemann feared, authentic Berlin would also disappear.

'Berlin white beer is, as its name indicates, a specifically Berlin drink, and consequently its peculiar nature and its qualities could be treasured and preserved only by "genuine Berliners". As the shape of the glasses and the nature of the beer forbade any hasty gulping down, leisure and comfort are the essential conditions of its enjoyment, and it is perhaps not untrue to say that its peculiar qualities reflect the comfortable, circumspect Philistine who was the typical *bourgeois* of old Berlin. What a contrast between an old beer-parlour in old Berlin and the great beer-palaces which have arisen since! In the one the citizen was an honoured guest; he was seated at a plain table in front of the big round glasses, reading a newspaper, or talking quietly and comfortably. In the other, eternal hurry and bustle, coming and going, folk barely leaving themselves time to sit down, and eating the customary roll on their feet or gulping down the half-pint of full beer and never taking their eyes from the clock, clearing out in a minute or two to make room for some one else who likewise hopes to "enjoy" a bite "in a hurry". It is interesting to note, and it is certainly not a mere coincidence, that in the very years in which Bavarian beer conquered Berlin, cigars in most sections of the community ousted the pipe. If we go just a short step farther and come to cigarettes we shall have to agree that the conditions necessary for the enjoyment of tobacco are very different, and that from the enjoyment of tobacco in one or other of its forms one may found very sound opinions on the character of the smokers, or at least on the circumstances under which they smoke'.

The heart of the two-and-twenty-year-old doctor is sore when he speaks of the passing of the class to which he belonged. Very seldom has a thesis been so personal, and it got more personal as it proceeded to its end. It deals with hundreds of details of beer-production, sale and finance, and finally comes to the activities of the retailer. How important, how responsible was his work! He got the beer from the brewery as 'fresh' beer; he let it ferment again in casks. It took great experience to fix the exact time for that operation. Then the yeast had to be drawn off. Then the beer was taken off in pails, again poured into casks, and mixed with fresh beer. The exact proportions of the mixture were different for each brewery, and to discover them was a difficult art.

'Many beer-retailers had a special reputation for excellent white beer.' That was his father's reputation.

But all that is over and done with. The doctoral thesis gives 'striking examples':

'Beer-retailer A. founded his business in 1866 in connexion with a public-house, and when the 'eighties commenced had two drays and four horses; one dray went out to deliver beer to the local bars. The turnover amounted to 50,000 marks annually. In 1893 he gave up the retail business, having lost practically all his custom and now is merely a beershop-keeper.

'Beer-retailer B., who has been in business since 1873, had formerly two horses and two drays. Now a handcart suffices. He now employs no hands.

'Beer-retailer C. had formerly two drays and three horses. The turnover amounted to 50,000 to 60,000 marks. Now he has one dray, one horse, and the turnover amounts to 20,000 marks. He has been in business since the 'sixties.

'Beer-retailer D. took over in 1891 the business belonging to E. E. required three drays and six horses and employed twelve hands. D. now needs only two horses in summer and one in winter. He still employs four hands. His business would have been completely ruined but for the fact that four military canteens are still his customers.

'Beer-retailer F., formerly employed twelve

hands and had a sale of from 10,000 to 12,000 hectolitres of beer annually. In hot weather he sold eighty half-barrels. When he died the business possessed only one dray. Under his widow the business went into bankruptcy.'

The list goes on to cite other examples. One can see that the candidate for honours in economics was a diligent collector of data. Who of these beer-retailers from A. to M. was his father? There is also something else that the reader of the thesis may see, and that is how fond this earnest student was of his own class. When later he became a middle-class politician—and he was a zealous one until foreign politics took him—when he creates organizations and puts forward laws intended to hinder the octopus expansion of capitalism, this is the explanation of his policy. His anti-materialist outlook comes from the romantic attachment to the lower middle class of his childhood. That was something very far removed from the ideals of the neo-Prussian youth of the epoch of Wilhelm II.

In his active career, however, Stresemann passed very quickly and surely from romance to prose. He made his way in industry. At twenty-two he was an assistant in the management of the Union of German Chocolate Manufacturers in Dresden. Then he was secretary to the Union of Manufacturers in the Dresden Area. At that period secretaries to business concerns did not invariably need to be doctors of economics. The Manufacturers' Union was an organization of the middle and small secondary industries, and stood in opposition to the German Industrialists' Association, representing the heavy industries, in political opposition both on tariffs and on social legislation. The 'die-hards' were in the Central Association; in the union it was freely said, 'Coalition against coalition, not soldiers against socialists.'

'It was not the worst elements of the working class that were able to attach less importance to the ordinary man's feeling that his own savings are the main thing than to the great idea of the solidarity of the working class. If I may draw a conclusion from this will to sacrifice on the part of the working class it would be to recommend to the employers that they devote the same will to sacrifice and energy to their own business and to their own political ideals, as the workers have done often under persecution and difficulties.'

The principle 'master in one's own house' he expressly rejected. Of the custom of many employers to deal with their own workers but not with an official of a trade union, he said, 'This point of view is simply not tenable.' The workers under it would only be 'postmen' who come from the union and again return to it. Therefore the union must be 'in one's own house' and must be recognized as the legitimate representative of the workers.

Stresemann founded a society for compensation when works closed down, that is to say, for insurance against strike losses. At this same period he joined the National Socialist League, the party of Friedrich Naumann, quickly recognized his mistake, and left it. From now on he stood throughout his career on the opposite side from Naumann. He went in the direction natural to him from his attitude to life and his claims upon it—to the National Liberals. Naumann is romance in politics. Prose leads the beginner to a strongly established party with fighting positions, with seats in Parliament, where it is possible to rise. At that time Stresemann was a slim, fair, young man with parted hair and a small moustache under the sharp nose, a genial, friendly soul, one who could hold his liquor and be brilliant, a good mixer—in fact, a real good fellow, who knew well how to talk over reluctant manufacturers mostly small employers. There is no trace yet of the powerful, hairless head, the full face with its big features which Hugo Lederer's bust will show some quarter of a century later. A keen, quick worker, a good organizer. Then he lays down the material foundations for his existence. He arranges for the foundation of a sugar factory outside the sugar ring so as to protect his chocolate manufacturers against the piracy of the sugar combine. Here he obtains his first directorship, the first of many.

CHAPTER II

THE WIDER WORLD

NOTHING is got for nothing, and least of all in the world which we now enter. The Dresden-Bautzen Association, to whose service the twenty-three-year-old Streseman had passed from that of the Chocolate Manufacturers' Association, had an annual budget of 5,000 to 6,000 marks —a mere nothing compared to the mighty armed leagues of the other German industries. In Leipzig there was a second tiny group just as insignificant. On January 15th Stresemann began work in Dresden. On February 21st the Dresden-Bautzen group had combined with the Leipzig group; the Association of Saxon Industrialists took their place. At the meeting which decided on amalgamation it was only with difficulty that an attendance of thirty-seven members was got together. Stresemann, as secretary, received a quarterly salary of 250 marks. Two years later the association had 7,000 members who employed 600,000 workers. Saxony served as model for Thuringia, Silesia, and Württemberg, where similar associations were set up. At the end of the war, forty to fifty thousand concerns were members of these associations.

This Saxon Association, which as a result of Stresemann's efforts became a power, was naturally in opposition to the Central Association of the heavy industries. The coal and iron magnates had already established their position by the side of the aristocracy. The secondary industries, which for the most part were represented by small concerns, started too late their opposition to the powerful businesses of the heavy industries. The policy of prices carried out by the coal combine made things difficult for them; the high tariff system and the system of monopolies strangled them. Stresemann took the offensive against these. In Saxony there were practically only secondary industries. As a result the land was ruled by the great landowners, who had been firmly in power since the days of feudalism. In the Upper House there were twenty-seven land-owners and not a single industrialist. Yet three-quarters of the population lived by industry and commerce and only a tenth on the land. The economic struggle became a political one.

Stresemann could not only be sweetly persuasive; he could also be unpleasantly truculent in controversy. One of his opponents who defended the prerogative of the gentry was the Chamberlain Sahrer von Sahr auf Ehrenberg—not even a poet could imagine a name more resonant. Stresemann sarcastically told him that if his proposals were accepted, the industrialists might expect admission to the hallowed floor of the Upper House somewhere about the year 2586. After fierce assaults on the Junkers' lines the Royal Government declared its readiness to allow industrialists to enter the Upper House. But things went no farther. The framers of the necessary law could not reach agreement on its contents. Until the flood of the revolution broke down the defences, the fortress of the magnates held out. Industry could make a victorious entry only to the Second Chamber.

Similar ideas inspired Stresemann when later on he sought to create a party of the small and middle industrialists, to which the bureaucracy might adhere, and also the *élite* of the workers, and which at the same time might represent the peasants against the great landowners. When he was Basserman's trusted lieutenant he sought to induce the National Liberal Party to create groups with allied economic interests. Bassermann saw only the objections to the scheme—the shattering of the painfully maintained party unity. He ignored the idea of the future, the idea of giving an economic basis to politics.

In all these activities Stresemann was consistent ; his views showed neither wavering nor changeableness. He opposed that development which appeared to divide society into big capitalists and propertyless proletarians. His policy was dictated by genuine feeling, and so he was true to it. He saw in his own youth how the beer-retailers fell before the great breweries. Even as Minister he was angered if combines treated the State as if it were something that did not matter. To one great industrial magnate who refused information about the plans of his combine he used the threat, 'We have no further need of you ; the State will take over your syndicate.' Socialization to him was the very devil. But he played it as a card against Beelzebub.

Stresemann recognized the relation of economics to politics ; his ambition led him to politics. In 1903 he helped at the elections. In 1906 he was a delegate to the National Liberal Party Conference at Goslar. He used the occasion, as it was the first that had offered, to make an attack on the party leadership.

The party was thunderstruck. For a quarter of a century unconditional loyalty to the Empire had been interpreted as unconditional loyalty to the Government. The Government had never had any anxiety about the National Liberals. It relied on them. 'You are a Government Party pure and simple,' cried the young orator to the grey-haired patriarchs who were his leaders. 'We are as strong a party in Parliament as the Conservatives, and how sadly our influence has declined in even personal questions—I mean, in the matter of the personnel of the Prussian administration—as compared with that powerful party.' And why this decline? The voice of the young man with the little moustache under the sharp nose quivered with emotion. 'The Government esteems the Conservative Party more highly because that party has many times energetically opposed it and said frankly, "We will not support you." The Liberal Party, a Government Party pure and simple, supporting a Conservative Government which the Conservative Party knows how to oppose!' The sharp-tongued young doctor asked the most honourable Herr Bassermann to his face why he was silent about abuses in the civil service, about ill-treatment in the barracks, about corruption in the colonies. From the heart of the party leader came a burst of anger: 'This is a scandal.' The recruit went on to a clarion appeal: 'Let us have more Liberalism and not just National Liberalism. Let us oppose, criticize, aspire to power.'

Unconditional adherence to the hierarchy, to this divinely appointed dependence, had reacted on the party. There were certainly young Liberals who made trouble. But they were half outside the party. They could be negotiated with. They did not count very much. This young man was in the very centre of the party, and from that position launched the bright arrows of rebellion. The fickle, the easily influenced, shouted approval. The majority of the loyal, loudly and with all the violence of conviction, shouted, 'Sit down! Sit down!'

Very wearied, overburdened with business and social duties, the leader of the Mannheim *bourgeoisie* sat in the evening in his room. He sent away his friends; he sent away his secretaries. Then he sent for the rebel who had said these 'scandalous things'. He sat with him for hours in confidential discussion over a bottle of champagne.

In 1906 Stresemann entered the municipal council of Dresden. In January 1907, at the elections in which the Bülow *bloc* won its great victory and the Government Parties literally wallowed in seats, he entered the Reichstag. He was then twenty-eight. A little before that he had married. His bride was Kathe Kleefeld, a member of a distinguished Jewish family, a woman of beauty, ambition, and ability, belonging to a higher social class than himself.

At that time Stresemann was an imperialist of the first water. But his imperialism was not that coolly calculated sort like that of the great industrialists. He loved Herwegh's lines: 'Thou art the great people, the hope of the world. So let go the anchor.' He headed one of his articles, 'Michael, hearken, the wind blows from the sea.' Of the colonies he said that they were 'part of Germany's soul'. There was nothing of selfish careerism about his imperialism; it was all sheer feeling. And as feeling was so warm, so overpowering, it was a positive obstacle to him when prosaic questions of detail arose. Leagues to him were a field of boiling activity—the Navy League, the Colonial League, the German Training Ship League, and then the Hansabund. His father-in-law Kleefeld was a Hanseatic merchant. He planned a German Association for World Commerce. The scheme came to nothing. From the small shop in the Kopenicker Strasse he had launched out into the wide sea of German expansion to make great voyages. The constituency which sent him to the Reichstag was composed in the main of workers—poor workers. Things were not going well, it was known, with the Saxon workers: they were poorer than their Rhineland or Berlin comrades. He told in a speech which he delivered to the Navy League at Cologne, just after the election, that he had been warned not to say too much about fleets and colonies. But at every meeting he had declared, 'I stand for the strengthening of the German Fleet. I shall vote for the estimates which will provide it.'

He was quickly assured, he said, how right he had been. 'I have never found more sympathetic understanding than in the plain man, and that proves to me how powerful is this national ideal. And, if I may say so, it is equally powerful in the hearts of our German workmen.' 'That the money for the colonies was not voted was enough'—so he described the success of Bülow's electoral calculations—'to reduce the Social Democrats to half their strength.' 'The Fatherland must be defended, and if what is necessary for its defence is not voted, not a single Social Democrat will be returned at next election.'

Such was the boast of the twenty-nine-year-old deputy. He believed that his argument for a coalition of the industrialists with representation for the interests of the workers was proved. The workers' rejection of imperialist ambitions he reckoned as of little moment; they were as little justified as significant. In January 1912 Annaberg undeceived him. He was defeated and lost the seat. In the same year he stood at a by-election for Greiz. Here too the Social Democrat was returned. One may wonder if the plain man was quite so approving of the naval-building programme as the young politician imagined.

The defeat of Social Democracy at the Bülow *bloc* elections of 1907 was the result simply of alliances on the second ballot. In 1912 it won all its seats back, and thirty more besides. The total figures told an even plainer tale. The way the constituencies were drawn had played its part. Since the foundation of the North German Confederation, under whose electoral scheme one deputy was allotted to every 100,000 of the population, the boundaries of the constituencies had not been altered. During the decades in which the solid *bloc* of the proletarian party was formed, nothing had been changed. The total polls showed no Socialist loss. In 1907 the Anti-Fleet Party had polled 200,000 more votes than before. In 1913 it polled 1,000,000 more. It became a party of

4,000,000, the strongest bastion of the International.

It is not to be said that Stresemann was wrong because he went wrong in his last prophecy. If the Fatherland needed defence and a party refused to vote war credits—a real test of that was never made. When the moment did come, from the extreme Right to the extreme Left the Reichstag stood united. The reason? The war was against Russia. Friedrich Engels in 1891 wrote: 'Then arise, if Russia begins war, arise, fall on the Russians and their allies whoever they are', and Bebel in the Reichstag said that if the order to march against the Tsar came, he himself would shoulder a rifle.

The young Stresemann took his seat in the Reichstag as a party rebel. He called the National Liberals 'a Government Party pure and simple', and preached to them the desire for power. Hence the cries of 'Sit down'; hence the applause; hence the midnight discussion with Bassermann; hence his candidature and election. The desire for power which he desired to see in the party he could now make his concern. Nothing would have been better for the Reichstag, nothing more salutary for the Empire. For what was the Reichstag in the Empire? What did it further? What did it hinder? What did it achieve?

Even before Stresemann entered Parliament—in 1905—there was an unpleasant affair which threatened grave danger to the Empire. The easily-excited Emperor had become enthusiastic over the idea of a Continental *bloc*. When he met the Tsar on the Baltic he half invited, half forced, him to come to an agreement. It was sheer improvisation without any sign of genius, without constitutional warrant. France was to be compelled by diplomatic action to adhere to the Russo-German Alliance which was to be made. Whenever 'the Treaty of Björkö' became known, Britain could not but take alarm. Wilhelm wrote triumphantly to Nicolas that at the mere rumour of the treaty Britain was in 'the wildest excitement'. The agreement made by the royal cousins was quietly and privately torn up by their ministers.

It was then that those who knew what was going on began to fear that the Imperial rule would end in catastrophe. The opinion was general that no further possibility of ruling so effectively should occur. The former deputy, Baron von Richthofen, has related how his father-in-law, the Under-Secretary in the Foreign Office, declared his conviction that only the introduction of the parliamentary system could prevent such enormities occurring. Even Holstein, the *eminence grise,* the secret master of the Wilhelmstrasse, held similar opinions. 'Left' and 'Right' conceptions did not enter into it at all. Richthofen was said to have Liberal leanings; Holstein certainly was not suspected of them. It was a question of 'to be or not to be' for the nation. If the Emperor was a danger to the Empire, then the nation must look for another source of power. Germany by its constitution was a constitutional State. The next foundation on which the nation could build was the Reichstag. But the Reichstag had no flash of illumination; no representative of the people had the slightest inkling that a dark cloud had gathered over it and had been dissipated.

The Imperial interview in the *Daily Telegraph*

was really more important than the Treaty of Björkö, because this time Wilhelm had spoken of his people's invincible dislike of the English, a dislike which he himself fought against in vain. Germany saw, and for a reason which was very far from reality, its relations with the British Empire threatened. In the Bundesrat, where the German princes were represented, the Emperor's abdication was considered. In his own family it was believed that the rage of the nation would drive him from the throne. The nation did not understand the Reichstag's methods. The parties, Bassermann at their head, made formal protest. But with a lame declaration from the Emperor that it would not occur again the whole incident came to an end. How was a recurrence of the incident to be prevented ? To win a right of control, to win influence, power, the Reichstag never rose to that. Now would have been the time for it to show will to power, the best opportunity the Wilhelm epoch ever afforded. The excitement died down. The *Telegraph* incident ended with Bülow's dismissal. Two years later Wilhem II, walking in the garden of the Imperial Chancellery with the King of Württemberg, stopped suddenly and said, ' Here was where I gave the rascal the sack.'

Stresemann's political history in these years is the history of Bassermann, the history of the National Liberal Party. Between its left wing and its right wing Bassermann constituted by himself a centre party in this party of the centre. He could lean on no one. In Stresemann a new power was arising, and the power that was in him was there for the leader to use. Stresemann was elected to the Reichstag in 1907. He stepped at once into the front rank. His speeches on the Home Office estimates aroused attention and were reported in many newspapers. The first, on the position of private employees, the *Tägliche Rundschau* called the high-water mark, the very essence of parliamentary tactics. In 1912 he was beaten twice at the polls. The leadership of the party was courting both the right wing and the left. Stresemann's youthful temperament seemed a danger to the right wing. In order again to isolate Bassermann, Friedberg, a professor, a privy councillor, leader of the party in the Prussian Parliament and fundamentally a Conservative, had the defeated deputy forced out of the executive committee, the real controlling power of the party. It was for Stresemann a year of political reverses. They wanted to be rid of him. He found salvation in another field. He took a trip to the United States and to Canada, where he spoke at the conference of the International Chamber of Commerce at Boston and before the United Chambers of Commerce at Toronto. The Hansabund, the Germano-Bulgar Association and the German-American Association employed him to found a German technical college in China and a German Association for World Trade, and with a scheme for a great news-agency, plans which never got any farther. Nothing solid was given him—no directorship, no important post in business, no real power to influence trade and industry. Stresemann was no child of fortune to whom things came of themselves. Soon he was personally attacked. His attempt to create an alliance between the Central Association and the League of Industrialists roused the opposition of the heavy industries and of the free traders alike. The *Frankfurter Zeitung* bitterly attacked him. And here too he first fell foul of Hugenberg. The Association for World Trade, a propaganda scheme of the widest range, collapsed. But, even if nothing came to him, he was still through all these years in the main stream of German Imperialist expansion. Industry, trade, the army, the fleet, colonies—was not everything well guided in the best of all worlds? Stresemann now lived in a big house in the Tauentzienstrasse in Berlin, close by the Memorial Church. His young wife was busied with her *salon*. Two sons, Wolfgang and Joachim, were growing up. His family happiness was the greater because his family life never was what the world calls interesting. A beautiful woman, who in the early years of the Republic was very active politically, is said to have said of him, 'The man is no leader for me. Why, even when we are alone he never thinks of talking of anything but politics.' Stresemann never had the least inclination to gallantry.

'We are young and that is splendid!' Goethe's words may well stand as the motto for his activity in these years.

CHAPTER III

WASTED HOURS

AS soon as the North German Confederation had been formed, the founder and first leader of the National Liberal Party, Rudolf von Bennigsen, had striven to obtain the parliamentary system. Since then there had come the Empire, political expansion, and the attainment of the rank of a world power, the frenzied development of industrial production, the giant increase in the export trade, the commercial fleet, the war navy, the new-gained wealth of the middle classes, the high wages of the workers, the supremacy of Germany in social legislation. Men were busied with other things than anxiety about the permanence of the Empire. The party leaders too were not at all of the opinion that they were without any influence on policy. When Hohenlohe was Chancellor, and still more under Bülow, the relations between Government and Parliament had become close, even intimate. The deputies were approached, appealed to, asked for advice, Bills were altered, withdrawn, put forward as they desired. The Conservative von Normann, the leader of the Reichspartei von Kardoff, the Centrist politician Peter Spahn, the National Liberal Bassermann—all of them had a weighty word to say. Parliament once went so far as to strike the provision for two army corps from the army estimates, and Ludendorff in his various apologies has assured us

time and again that the non-existence of these corps was the reason why the war was not won. But the German Parliament was allowed to say nothing on questions of army leadership, which was the exclusive province of the supreme war lord, with his divinely granted right of command, nor on foreign policy, whose secrets were carefully concealed from it, nor on State appointments. The high, and even the highest, places were filled without the deputies being consulted; in such business they were not allowed to meddle. The representatives of the German people had no voice in those final decisions on which the fate of the German people depended. To the student Stresemann the National Liberal Party seemed to have become too governmental. But the Reichstag as a whole was governmental, and when in 1907 the Centrists joined those enemies of the State, the Social Democrats, to reject the colonial estimates, then the eternally critical Progressives made strait alliance with the parties that were 'loyal to the State', and at the elections the alliance gave a brilliant victory to the Imperial Government. Even the electors were governmental. The splendid opportunity to provoke a constitutional crisis was lost in 1907 just as in 1908. Neither opportunity produced a man who could use it.

It was Erzberger who had unleashed the colonial controversy. This schoolmaster from Buttenhausen in Württemberg had the temperament of a fighter. His capacity for work was gigantic; he was a master of the art of convincing and was strongly inclined to take an independent line. After his murder Stresemann passed judgement upon him in words unaffected by sentimental considerations: 'Erzberger had a quite unusual capacity for hard work and also a savage regardlessness which was peculiar to him and by which he carried through whatever he undertook to a triumph from which finer spirits would have shrunk.' He placed Erzberger's development in still clearer contrast to his own when he said, ' He did not take the path which would have made him the trusted lieutenant of a chief under whose guidance he could have worked himself into a second place in political life. He acknowledged no leadership but his own and trod a lonely path. In the Reichstag the story went that during the whole recess in which deputies avoid parliamentary work, Herr Erzberger used to appear with the dawn, read through all the parliamentary papers, compare all the estimates and so formidably equip himself with facts as to make himself inevitably a leader in the debates on the estimates next session. He led, it was said, and with truth, the life of an ascetic. He did not like company. He worked sixteen hours a day and built up that command of nerve which made him fit to stand in the front line of battle without losing his composure under the hottest fire.'

Thus Stresemann drew the picture of the man who had before him been the Benjamin of the Reichstag and whom he had once considered as an opponent, as a competitor in the struggle for power. It was one of Erzberger's qualities that he could swiftly respond to suggestions. But he had the defects of his qualities. He fell easily under any influence that touched him. The clever men of the Foreign Office, of the War Office, of the Admiralty—these were the cleverest—soon got to know his weakness. Why trouble oneself with the older generation of parliamentarians to get them to influence the younger? They went directly to the younger elements, spoke them fair, and made them docile. Foreign diplomacy perhaps did not always function successfully; Parliamentary diplomacy never failed to function brilliantly.

When one considers Erzberger's activity, it is difficult to decide whether it was aimed at increasing the power of Parliament or simply his own power as a parliamentarian. It was so in the years before the war, and the difficulty persists all through the war years. When the struggle for power reached its crisis in the summer of 1917 the question was settled. Then Parliament won because Erzberger attacked. But even earlier, especially in the colonial controversy of 1906–7 and in the years following, he was an animating force. He was not the only one influential in this sense, but he was the most alive, the busiest, the richest in ideas, the readiest to take the initiative. Other young deputies too wanted to stop the peaceful but dangerous game of playing up to the Government which the older generation played, for instance the National Liberals, Baron von Richthofen and Schiffer, the Centrist deputy Martin Spahn. Stresemann remained in the background, As we know, he was inclined to be a rebel. But he indulged his inclination only in matters of secondary importance, for instance on the proportion of aristocrats to *bourgeois* in the diplomatic service. That was certainly not an unimportant question, but it was not the main question. And he completely ignored the main question when in 1910 he raised the matter in the Reichstag. From that subject it would have been easy to have passed to attack the three-class electoral system in Prussia, the composition of the Prussian Upper House, the officering of the guards and the cavalry of the line with nobles, the Prussian bureaucracy. In his speech at the Goslar Conference he had loudly complained that the administration had been handed over to the Conservatives and that the National Liberal Party bore this patiently. Now he did not go so far. He was what Gogol would call a nice sort of rebel. He tried no tricks, as did Erzberger, the terror of his party leader. He remained in the wake of Bassermann, who by stumping the country secured an increase in the army estimates without ever showing what was going to be done with the army corps he had obtained. It was the task of the National Liberals to look after the greatness of the Empire, to secure the necessary funds for the Empire's rulers. Thus they conceived their mission, and they fulfilled it. But they did not trouble themselves to ask whether the use of the funds obtained would bring prosperity or destruction to the Empire. Of the efforts of the British Minister, Haldane, who came in 1912 to Berlin to try to come to an agreement with Germany on the question of naval construction, Bassermann and Stresemann must have been aware. The Conservatives, who as believing Prussian royalists could leave responsibility to the King of Prussia, were in quite a different position. The National Liberals as constitutionalists, as successors of Bennigsen and as descendants of the men of the Paulskirche, must take responsibility on themselves. But Bassermann wrote a pamphlet in honour of Tirpitz ; he stood by his dangerous building programme. Bismarck used to lie awake o' nights when the nightmare of coalitions appalled him. Did that nightmare never trouble the slumber of the National Liberal leaders? They never took a decisive step—or at least only one decisive step—to get rid of it. Bassermann was the first party leader to interpellate the Government when the *Daily Telegraph* interview threatened to disturb Germany's relations with Britain. But that was only party criticism. To pass from negative criticism to positive influence on the course of foreign policy—the Reichstag never once girded up its loins to that. Peter Spahn, the aged Centrist leader, and his son Martin, who to-day is a member of the Nationalist Party, discussed these matters once; it was in 1909. The son said, 'We get no farther with this inefficiency. You will see that you will be left behind!' The father replied, 'There is no other way. You young men must think of the position of the German Empire as it is now. All is brittle as glass, so brittle that only with extreme care can we proceed from incident to incident, from statesman to statesman.'

It was Bassermann's opinion, too, that everything was 'brittle as glass'—unhappily for that theory 1918 showed that there was nothing brittle about the German nation—and that therefore the Reichstag could not make the strong effort that was necessary to obtain control over the national affairs. That would have been possible only in a struggle with the Conservatives and in alliance with the Social Democrats. The Centre Party did not shrink from that alliance when in 1906 it was concerned ostensibly about colonial policy, but in reality with securing power to influence the Government. For Bassermann that was against all decency; it was positively immoral. As far as the National Liberals were concerned, political activity meant propaganda in favour of Imperialist policies and defence of them against the anti-Imperialist Social Democrats. If Stresemann later displayed extreme courage and initiative, it is all the more necessary to remember how terribly the crisis before the war demanded a man of courage and that Stresemann did not come forward as the man required. The call to the wide world with its unlimited possibilities for the Empire bewitched him. He himself later on made answer to his critics: 'One forgets the feeling of security by which one was lulled so long, forgets that we inherited from the Bismarck period a habit of placing in his successors the trust we had in him, the trust he had so richly deserved, and that therefore to influence foreign policy was very difficult.' Of the mission of Hoyos to Berlin, of the discussions at Potsdam, of the *carte blanche* which Wilhelm II gave the Ballplatz—no member of Parliament knew anything.

Bassermann, captain in the Landswehr cavalry, went to the front to take command of an ammunition train. Stresemann went at the outbreak of war to Dresden. In December he was elected member for Aurich and returned to Berlin and to Parliament. He was never in the army. The army doctors found that his heart was not strong enough for service. There never was any question of his being called up. His party leader came home on leave and turned ill. He could not attend to business. Stresemann was his man of confidence and became *de facto* leader of the party. Still more than before was his activity many-sided, extended, full of zeal. He became Vice-Chairman of the Industrial Committee, on which the secondary and the heavy industries, the League, and the Central Association were represented side by side. These were the days of those speeches and articles which were collected under the title 'Michael, Hear, the Sea Wind Blows' —clarion calls to rouse the heart, to maintain enthusiasm. With others, he founded the 'Wednesday Association', a famous body in which, as the Press was under censorship, serious and confidential exchanges of opinion took place. His importance, his reputation increased. His name became known.

The Reichstag spent three of the war-years in work for the years after the war. Thereafter things would be different; the labour of the nation in the trenches, the granting of the credits would then all be paid for. The struggle with the powers that were—that was for the future. The present was surrendered to them. The Social Democrats demanded the appointment of a commission on the Constitution. Under Stresemann's leadership the National Liberals did the same. In this case Stresemann acted independently; he went counter to Bassermann's wishes. In the Constitutional Commission there was demanded responsibility of the Chancellor and the Secretaries of State to Parliament, the counter-signature by the Minister of War of officers' commissions, manhood suffrage as for the Reichstag for the State parliaments. Equally, the parliamentary system, the abolition of the Emperor's right of command, the destruction of the fortress of the Prussian aristocracy. Stresemann took the fight against the existing Prussian franchise seriously. He did not reckon it a light matter to be

ON THE WAY TO THE LEAGUE MEETING

A PHOTOGRAPH TAKEN AT GENEVA SHOWING HERR STRESEMANN AND (RIGHT) STATE SECRETARY VON SCHUBERT

compelled to go against his party comrades. He must sacrifice them, for the strength and position of the National Liberal Party in the Prussian Parliament was threatened if the plutocratic franchise was abolished. The National Liberals were, after all, 'the party of culture and property'. Hence an intense effort to convince them. 'The overwhelming majority of the party members considers that a reasonable unequal franchise is fundamentally the best system. For the party the recognition of the necessity from the point of view of the State of the introduction of manhood suffrage is an outrage on their better judgement; for the loyal party man it means a weakening of his party and the excessive strengthening of groups with which the party has never been able to co-operate ever so slightly in the political field.' That meant even at that date the Social Democrats. But the argument proceeded: 'It would not be difficult to produce thousands of knights of the Iron Cross who stand for the equal franchise. Such men you cannot disperse by calling out your militia or your policemen.' He even tried later, but with little success, to convince Ludendorff.

Meantime Parliament was without influence on what was happening at the moment and did not try to obtain it. Stresemann wrote, 'One ought not to expect that the Constitution of Germany can be changed like a garment overnight!' And 'there has been no lack of efforts to drive the majority parties in the Reichstag to power and to demonstrate to them that the time has come when they must take control of the Government and be able to give expression to the will of the majority of the representatives of the people. Such a majority Government in war-time does not seem to me to be practicable.' The driving force—that was Erzberger. Stresemann's attitude can hardly be described as resignation; it was too negative, too vague. It was merely renunciation of power. The fate of Germany was in the balance and the Reichstag was only a spectator.

But the Constitution, not the written one but the real one, had meantime been profoundly changed. With Ludendorff as the soul of Army Head-quarters the whole scene changed. His appointment was an unprecedented, a revolutionary event. The Emperor was simply shouldered aside. Well had he once groaned: 'If I could only never have to see that drill-sergeant again', but, timid soul as he really was, he was lucky then to be let live without anxiety. Chancellor and high officialdom were driven into the background, on to the defensive. They had to defend themselves against the Bills, the projects, which Ludendorff forwarded to them, or bring them in themselves. The feeding of the nation profoundly influenced the feeling of the army, and so was a military concern. It was the same with political reform. War aims, annexations, had to be decided from the strategic point of view, and so required to be judged by the Army Command. The overwhelming majority of the Reichstag took delight in this change of system. No one had any confidence in Bethmann-Hollweg as the shaper of Germany's future; Bassermann was hostile to him; Stresemann's opposition was still stronger; he despised the fifth Imperial Chancellor. As his only service Bethmann, when he left office, spoke proudly of his achievement in getting the Social Democrats to retract their denial of the State. Stresemann's own character is revealed in this dislike. He did his best to do justice to the Chancellor, but the effort was too much for him. Purity of intention and love of country, these are qualities one expects of men in the service of the State. But purity of intention never prevented Bethmann from taking improper action when he thought his own person was endangered. Stresemann certainly thought him malicious, and said so plainly. He was always listening to gossip. scenting intrigues, and, if he got but a whiff of one, answered with an intrigue of his own.

Bassermann had telegraphed to his party associate, the Bavarian councillor von Buhl, that 'the long one' was ripe for overthrow, and asked him to influence 'his master', the King of Bavaria, to have him removed. The telegram got to Bethmann, who managed to decipher it. He summoned leading members of the National Liberal Party to prove to them that their party chief was a danger to the State. Stresemann never forgave him for that. That the Imperial Chancellor should seek to asperse party leaders and behind their backs conduct a palace revolution, he considered disgraceful.

In February, 1917, the dismissal of the Chancellor was demanded of the Emperor. Conservative and National Liberal deputies, industrialists, and merchants were invited to the Adlon Hotel to hear a lecture from Stresemann 'on the state of the chemical industry'. A draft of the appeal to the Emperor was enclosed with the card of invitation. The Progressive deputy, Haussmann, got wind of the plot and put an alarmist news paragraph in the

Berliner Tageblatt. This brought down the conspiracy.

Stresemann disliked the dry manner that was peculiar to Bethmann. He disliked the lecturer in him ; the ' learned politician ' might go down with many, but not with him. The admission that the violation of Belgian neutrality was contrary to international law, the tears which he had shed to the British Ambassador, all that was painful to Stresemann, angered him. The harsh earnestness of the man, the joylessness, the ascetism of his life he could not abide. Stresemann was essentially a cheerful liver. He drank wine, he loved students' songs, lively argument, colour, and movement ; he was as much at home at the Stage Club as at the Seppel in Heidelberg. This long and lengthy man who could not laugh properly was his opposite. Everything came to Bethmann through long reflection, deliberation, deduction. With Stresemann it was the heart which spoke ; all was exuberance, warmth. The policies they pursued were not antagonistic ; for the most part they were the same policy. It was intensity of feeling that divided them. Bethmann, as is known, was also haughty. He regarded the young deputy with the brilliant oratorical gifts as a demagogue, perhaps let him see that he did regard him as such. That Bethmann, when it came to action, to co-operation with others, was no national leader, that he placed on others the responsibility for his own defects was to Stresemann unpardonable. ' There is nothing more pitiable,' he wrote, ' than a political government which runs about with streaming eyes because it is dominated by the military authorities. People either should not let themselves be dominated, or should resign their posts.'

Stresemann set up the army leaders for reverence in place of the despised Chancellor. When in the Budget Commission electoral reform and the introduction of the parliamentary system were being debated, Stresemann proposed that Hindenburg and Ludendorff should be invited to attend. It was Bethmann who opposed: 'But, gentlemen, I must expressly warn you against making the Army Command directly a factor in political life.' That was mere dissimulation. The Army Command for long had not only been a factor, but had been the most influential factor in politics. But if Parliament was directly connected with the Army Command, then the Imperial Chancellor was eliminated. He counted as no more than a messenger. With his proposal Stresemann hit the nail on the head. It corresponded exactly to the actual situation. But it showed no will to power, only a desire to increase the power of the Army Command.

It is impossible to judge Ludendorff's personality rightly if he is regarded simply as people regard him to-day. One must take the trouble to reconstruct what he meant to that generation. He exercised enormous influence on all who came in contact with him. It is said that a disease of the thyroid gland has affected his mind since the war. But during the war he was the personification of energy, and had to work with a weak generation, with an officers' corps which grew no farther in stature than to that of a regimental commander, with a monarch who was a broken man, and a people that had not yet arrived at the stage of thinking for itself. Amid puppets, sycophants, dodderers, and puffed-up nonentities, he seemed to be verily 'the man'. The source of strength and power, Stresemann called him in admiration. He broke into one domain after another of the national life. Stresemann had willingly surrendered to him. A political opponent tells us that once in 'the cynical lobbies' Stresemann was called 'Ludendorff's young man'. It was believed that a direct line connected the study of the deputy with that of the general. Actually their personal relations were anything but close. But how deep was his devotion to the general was revealed by a letter which he wrote to him on April 29, 1918. He asked that the Army Command would not hinder the dissolution of the Prussian Parliament if the equal franchise were rejected. He wrote that 'the majority of July 19th had broken down under the swift growth of the sentiment of victory'. He was proud to be one of those who 'in hundreds of meetings had stood for the unlimited authority of the Army Command'. He warns Ludendorff off home politics, but unconditionally surrenders to him the field of foreign politics. 'In all the great questions of foreign policy on which the views of the Army Command must be of decisive significance, the memorable confidence which at present the Army Command enjoys would be lessened, and the fruits of that lessening would be gathered by the advocates of a peace of renunciation.' The best evidence that no close relations existed between the deputy and the general is in Ludendorff's answer: 'You know that I think only of a successful end to the war, and that I only give an opinion to the Imperial Government on home politics, however deeply these may move me, when

I believe that they may compromise that final success. My action is determined by these principles.' Seven lines of answer to five pages of typescript, and the matter worthy of the Pythia herself!

During these years Ludendorff's photograph stood in Stresemann's study; his romantic need of hopefulness, of belief in victory was so compelling that he grappled himself to this bulwark of victory with hooks of steel, sure that this was a great man, the single man of action and achievement. Then all must be staked upon him. When strong and passionate desires fill the heart the critical faculties are hampered.

The National Liberal leaders, when the war took them by surprise, were pessimistic. The Secretary of State, von Jägow, had laid it down to Bassermann and other deputies that the aim of German policy must be to get quit of this most unfortunate of wars as rapidly as possible. 'Both Throne and Empire are at stake'; Stresemann had heard that a score of times from Bassermann. In the first years of the war the many partial successes blinded their vision. Only three deputies of the party persisted in their scepticism — Prince von Schönaich-Carolath, Dr. Junk, and Baron von Richthofen. In the spring of 1917 Richthofen and Erzberger went on a tour to the eastern front. They met General Hoffman, the chief of the General Staff of the Eastern Command, an officer who right to the end of the war maintained his independence of view. The result of their conversations was that they brought back a fundamentally different conception of the war from that which prevailed in Germany and the Reichstag generally. Besides, Erzberger knew of the communication from the Austro-Hungarian Foreign Minister, Czernin, in which he had declared that the condition of his country was catastrophic and that peace must be made before the year was out. Erzberger was the man who made this new conception the basis for action. He said publicly, 'I place myself at the head of the opposition.' On July 6th he delivered his great speech in the Main Commission of the Reichstag. There was no longer justification for optimism; the Reichstag must find some way whereby Germany could get rid of the war. The excitement was intense, and Hindenburg and Ludendorff hurried to Berlin. The Kaiser arrived, asked what it was all about, and, coached by Bethmann, asked the astonished generals if their presence was not more urgently needed at the front. That was Bethmann's last vain effort. The Crown Prince came, and the generals came a second time. A majority was created in the Reichstag, composed of Social Democrats, Progressives, and Centrists. At first the National Liberals joined it, and then went out of it again. There was much talk of introducing the parliamentary system as if it might come the very next day. The Emperor announced the decision to grant equal, direct and secret suffrage to Prussia. On July 19th the peace resolution was carried in which it was declared that the words of the speech from the Throne on August 4th, 1914 still held good. 'No lust of conquest drives us on.' The Reichstag sought a peace of understanding and the permanent reconciliation of the peoples. Compulsory surrender of territory and political, economic, or financial domination were contradictory thereto. The National Liberals made a declaration which amounted to the same thing, but stressed the importance of Germany's military success.

Erzberger's speech was to Stresemann a terrible shock. He nearly broke down altogether. Payer says that he was absolutely ' aghast '. In the forenoon of July 7th he had an interview with Erzberger and Colonel Bauer of the Army Command. To the Secretary of State, Helfferich, he said that he would have to tell his party that Ludendorff believed the war would be lost if Bethmann remained Chancellor. At the session of the Commission on July 10th he violently attacked the Chancellor and demanded his resignation. Bassermann was then very ill; he died a week later. Peter Spahn was absent; he had had a stroke.

On July 11th the Crown Prince invited deputies to come and see him. Friedrich von Payer, the leader of the Progressive Party, says: ' As far as I am aware it was the first time in five-and-forty years that a representative of the Prussian monarchy had felt the need of informing himself of the views of the party leaders in the Reichstag.' Payer was certain that besides himself only deputies believed to be hostile to the Chancellor would be invited. It was not really a case of obtaining objective opinions from the guests whom the Crown Prince had invited; it was a case of getting material for a political intrigue. The scene was grotesque. In the background were officers taking a shorthand note, among them Colonel Bauer, the political agent of the Army Command and the arranger of this very meeting. The Crown Prince put clearly formulated questions.

Was a change in the Chancellorship necessary? Or was it not necessary? To Erzberger he said, 'Turn the fellow out in the Reichstag.' As if it was at a recruits' parade, says Payer, 'the man next the deputy who was being talked to' already stood to attention, to make sure that no valuable time was lost. Erzberger, Payer, Stresemann, the Social Democrat David, and Martin from the Economic League.

That was the second act of the drama.

The decision came during the interval. After Stresemann's attack on the Chancellor and the questioning of the deputies by the Crown Prince, Bethmann on the 11th submitted his resignation to the Emperor, who refused it. Thereupon the generals, on their side, on the 12th, demanded to be relieved. Here was a new constitutional development, a revolutionary event that Prussian officers should ask to be relieved in face of the enemy, a complete transformation of what was held to be the most conservative, apparently the most stable, the most unshakable, part of the constitution, the military. On the 13th Baron von Maltzan, a Prussian deputy and political adjutant to the Crown Prince, collected written declarations from the parties that they did not wish the Chancellor to be maintained in power. When early on the 14th Hindenburg and Ludendorff again arrived in Berlin, Bethmann had already fallen. At once the Prussian Food Controller and Under-Secretary of State, Michaelis, was appointed to succeed him. No member of Parliament knew beforehand of this appointment. It is said that once in the Prussian Parliament Michaelis had declared that 'no one should stay his arm ', and that this remark had drawn the attention of the military to him. Michaelis was in Berchtesgaden when the summons came to him. Like a good Christian he opened his Bible to obtain guidance. Where it opened there was a verse which seemed to counsel acceptance. He accepted.

The third act was played out in the offices of the General Staff. Scheidemann called it ' military trial by the Army Command '. Privy Councillor Jungheim, the director of the Reichstag, brought invitations ' for the gentlemen of the Progressive Party at 5 o'clock, the Centrists at 5.15, the Social Democrats at 5.30 '. Then came National Liberals, Anti-Semites, Conservatives. Ludendorff outlined the military situation to the deputies. A Russian victory possible only if Austria gives way. Otherwise the risk of it infinitesimal. (There was a battle at Luck which was no inconsiderable reverse.) In the west the line held firm.

There was no tonnage for the American troops. In March as a result of the U-boat campaign England would be ready for peace. (According to the Admiralty's earlier estimates, at the end of 1916 England's readiness for peace was already long overdue.) The peace resolution was not admired, but nevertheless it was accepted. Only a little sub-editing would be asked. ' More pepper, gentlemen, more pepper,' said the Field-Marshal. On July 12th he had asked the Emperor ' to tell the Government to prevent any such resolution passing ' ; the resolution ' would shatter the offensive power and the capacity for resistance of the army '.

The end of the play was the reception of leading

deputies, except Independent Socialists, by the Emperor on July 20th at tea. Erzberger has told us what happened. 'The party representatives were duly lined up by the Imperial Chancellor Michaelis and the Vice-Chancellor Helfferich and presented to the Emperor, who addressed a few remarks to each of them. . . . To every one's surprise the Emperor said that it was excellent that the Reichstag desired "a compromise peace".' (The Reichstag resolution, however, did not contain that very equivocal phrase so steadily demanded by the Army Command.) '"The word compromise is excellent; he discovered it", and the Emperor pointed to Vice-Chancellor Helfferich, who was engaged in passing round cigarettes. "Compromise consists in this, that we shall take from our enemies money, raw materials, cotton, coal, oil, and transfer all that from their pockets to ours. Assuredly it is a most excellent word." The members of the majority parties saw with horror that the Emperor had never been informed what their real wishes were, and they felt that these words were mere cruel mockery of them. Further, the Emperor said that it was true that the present war would not end with the defeat of England, but, at the end of it, there would be a far-reaching understanding with France and under his leadership the whole Continent would wage the real war, the war against England, which he called "the second Punic war". Our consternation increased. Passing, then, to the battle which had been fought some days before in Galicia the Emperor said that under the command of his son Fritz, the Prussian Guard had smashed up the Russians, "the democratic riffraff from the west. Where the Guard arrives there is no democracy". These were his actual words. Then turning towards us, he spoke of the certainty of the success of the submarines on which I had expressed doubt. England's east coast was but a vast graveyard of ships. In two or three months England would be finished. In Australia four million tons of foodstuffs were ready, but England could not transport them. In conclusion he said, "My officers tell me that now they never meet ships on the high seas flying the enemy flag." I observed that if that was so I could not understand how the Admiralty could announce that 600,000 tons of enemy shipping were sunk each month. With a gesture of annoyance, the Emperor turned his back on me. That evening aged deputies who till then would have nothing to do with parliamentary reform said openly that the system that at present ruled in Germany would bring only misfortune. Alas, strength of character was lacking to take the necessary decisions. In almost twenty years this was the first interview which the Emperor had with the representatives of the people; it was also the last.'

The new Chancellor Michaelis wrote of the reception in a letter to the Crown Prince: 'The deputies were very pleased and satisfied.'

. . . . .

Something extraordinary had taken place in the political life of Germany. A marvellous opportunity for a politician to realize great ends had passed. Much could have been altered, much could have been ended, much begun. In the end nothing happened at all, except that the strength of the opposing forces had become clear, precise, obvious. At the moment of crisis the political situation was fully revealed. Erzberger's attack had apparently been directed against the Chancellor. Actually it was against the Army Command. It was the latter which had to answer for the military situation, and the military situation was also the foreign political situation. The discussion turned on war aims. War aims also were the concern of the generals. Even public mention of them was controlled by them, for the censorship was in the hands of the military. It was Stresemann who first drew the consequences of Erzberger's demand, that the Chancellor must go. The Minister of War and some of his colleagues took up the hunt. They declared that Bethmann-Hollweg's past made him an unsuitable person to conclude a peace such as the Reichstag majority desired. The Army Command carried it further. The Crown Prince was no more than a message-boy whom Colonel Bauer engaged to run the errands of the generals. It was they too who ended the episode. They allowed a man to be made a Minister whom they believed to be compliant, and they shook hands with the Social Democratic leaders. When Erzberger delivered his speech in the Main Commission the excitement in the restricted circles which constituted what is called public opinion was intense. That is comprehensible. He had told the truth, and nothing is so upsetting, so revolutionary in its effects at a time when organized mendacity has unrestricted domination. If the military situation was not brilliant, as its official representatives declared it was, but was actually as Erzberger said threatened with disaster, then the system must be altered. And if the actual authority failed then the country must return to the veritable source of power. That was not the Prussian army as it had been in the days before Bismarck's conflict with the Reichstag. The Prussian army no longer existed ; the German army at the front, on the lines of communication, on the home defences, was the nation in arms. But the direct representative of that nation was the Reichstag. Thus when Erzberger had finished in every heart and on every lip the idea was present that the parliamentary system had arrived. Leadership and responsibility must be assumed by the Reichstag. The conception of the political situation which produced that thought was a correct one. But it was not the thought of the deputies ; their excitement was too great for that.

The true politician is more than any other a man of feeling. Only by the strength of his feeling can he be a leader, can he secure the co-operation of others. Clarity of apprehension is often greater in people who stand aside from politics than in the political leader. The political leader becomes a statesman only when apprehension is wedded to overwhelming feeling. The moment of this development in Stresemann's case had not yet come. It is said of him that among the excited he was the most excited, that he was out of himself, that he was 'struck all of a heap'. To apprehend the situation correctly in such circumstances means a flash of genius, a gift from Heaven. Then the gift was withheld.

Stresemann's collapse is explained by what had happened before the truth dawned on him. If the military position was bad, then it was the generals who were responsible for the appalling self-deception of the German people, of which he himself had been victim. The very possibility upset his soul, threatened his mental balance, deprived him of his self-command. Every instinct revolted against the growing conviction that he had been wrong. His feeling that the soldiers were good, the Chancellor bad, had been firm as a rock. Over against the realization that had dawned upon him as Erzberger spoke, there raised itself in opposition the belief that he was fast losing, that under such generals victory was certain, that only the political leaders could destroy it, only diplomacy make it of no avail. In the threatened collapse of his reasoning faculties he grasped at the means of salvation which offered themselves of their own accord in the conviction so clearly and so often reasoned and so constantly expressed. The routine of the parliamentarian like the often-tested adroitness of the debater reinforced his means of salvation from a mental catastrophe. He pressed on in the old direction, his goal was familiar, the arguments, a thousand times used in thought, came easily to him. Like an owl in daytime blindness, Stresemann blundered into the attack on the Chancellor, a man who was apart from the people, a statesman incapable of inspiring them, a bureaucrat born without the gift of leadership. Only years later did a sense of reality conquer in the politician ; now romance won the victory and held its gains under the severest ordeal.

In the case of others who received the same shock but who gathered strength to meet it things were different. Ludendorff was concerned to defend himself. Stresemann's error was actually a service to him and that he used it is comprehensible. The Emperor, weak whenever danger threatened, surrendered. He thought of the request of his generals to be relieved and knew that he could not do without them. How could a King of Prussia who was exactly what tradition said he should be have treated with his officers ? But Wilhelm had never been such a king. All ended on excellent good terms, even in jollity. Bethmann, whom no one loved, was sent into the wilderness. The army leaders went contentedly back to headquarters. Erzberger believed that he had created a basis for a possible peace conference. How little he abode by his own resolution was seen when he found the peace treaties of Brest and Bukarest to be in perfect agreement with it, when he assured the nation that with it as a basis, Briey and Longwy could be annexed to the Empire. The new Chancellor Michaelis wrote to the Crown Prince, 'On this resolution one can make any sort of peace one likes.' The parties believed that they had taken a step towards the winning of power. That too was delusion ; the respective strengths of the opposing forces had not varied by a finger breadth. The positive result was that the majority had indicated itself as a force which could change the holders of power if a revolutionary situation again arose. The front was formed. The 'Weimar coalition' was created in 1917.

With 'Right' and 'Left' Stresemann had little to do, as the struggle over the peace resolution showed. Stresemann was not 'Right' when he was a partisan of the Army Command. Erzberger, who, in the summer of 1918, was erecting thrones in the East and seeking to turn Liechtenstein into a State of the

Church, was therefore not a 'Left' politician. In July 1917 the Social Democrats had not stood in the front rank in the battle; they were not the offensive element. That was composed of the young deputies of the centre parties, Erzberger particularly, then Richthofen and others. Stürmer and Protopopoff, rank reactionaries, wanted to make peace with Germany. Miliukoff, Lvoff, Hessen, all constitutional democrats, and the Socialist Kerenski, wanted to fight the war to the bitter end. Erzberger's action had two sides to it. It offered two possibilities. It could serve the defeatists just as it could serve the annexationists. There were four combinations possible. Every patriot, Conservative or Social Democrat, could, as a result of it, come to desire peace at any price, not merely by a renunciation of Belgium and the conquests in the East, but also by the sacrifice of Alsace and Lorraine. The pessimistic Czernin was an arch-Conservative. On the other hand, every patriot, monarchist or republican, could arrive at the clear conclusion: we have been badly defended; let us defend ourselves better. Lloyd George and Clemenceau, who in a similar situation had both devoted themselves with the greatest energy to increasing their activities, were Left Radicals. Only in Germany was it possible for this mistaken conception of 'Left' and 'Right' to arise. The soldiers were freer from the error than the politicians. When Stresemann proposed to Ludendorff—this was before the days of the peace resolution—to make a Social Democrat Minister of Munitions, the general had no objection to offer. What he did say was, 'Why not, if the fellow can get us shells?' And indeed the only thing that could be said against it was the unfortunate mental reservation that was so common. In every respect the situation—if only it could be used—was one especially favourable for a politician whose nationalism was above suspicion. Scheidemann who on July 11, 1917 noted in his diary: 'The greater the distress, the higher rises the power of Parliament over the Government', would, just because he held to such a conception, be seriously hampered in an effort to organize the national defence. For he would have had to reverse his ideas, and with the rise in power of the Reichstag make the distress, and above all the danger, less. The politics of the day looked to the days after the war.

Rathenau had assured the supply of raw materials. He had advocated the deportation of Belgian workers; even in October 1918 he wanted to appeal to a *levée en masse*. In spite of all that no one ever considered him a reactionary. Gambetta was a Radical republican. Bülow gave it as his opinion: If no peace can be made, then we must 'draw the reins tighter at home' as had happened in France, and 'war to the knife'. In July 1917 an unprecedented opportunity was offered to a politician if, from Erzberger's revelations, he had drawn the conclusion that Germany must gather herself together for new, for heroic, efforts. In spite of a diet of turnips, in spite of empty grates, there was a possibility of fanning yet higher the flame of war-enthusiasm. That politician would have had to begin by tearing aside the veil which the military censor had hung between the nation and the truth. He would have to have cried out, 'We are lost if we are not braver, not more resolute, not readier for action.' The military apparatus was benumbed, bureaucratized. The feudal professionalism of the old army still worked to its detriment. Young and active officers sat peacefully on the staffs, on the lines of communication, in the home forces ; orders to the contrary were not carried out. Brave soldiers who had had no high school education were not given commissions. The companies were led by high school boys who had learned all they knew of war in hasty courses. The methods of distributing medals and decorations made the troops bitter. Everywhere favouritism aroused hostility. In the home defence forces villainy and corruption were rife. The system of supplies was functioning in a disorderly fashion ; the control of prices was a cause of unfair enrichment ; together with the escape from adequate taxation of war profits it added to the discontent. The list makes no claim to completeness. Defects were apparent everywhere in the military sphere. A real national leader would have at least had partially to reform it. In his war against inefficiency he could have roused the mass of the nation to new strength. Such a national leader could base himself only on the Reichstag. He would have had in the first place to turn against the powers that were who were responsible for rustiness and degeneracy. But the power that was responsible for both was not the Chancellor but the Army Command. From the former the power had long since passed ; it had fallen to the generals.

The way in which the Germans stated the problem was false. Consequently they could find no solution. The so-called war-aims were all right for café tables at home and for the higher staffs.

For the masses, in so far as they were not absolutely exhausted, the issue was one of victory or defeat, not of the occupation of Liège, or of annexation of the iron deposits, or of the incorporation of the Baltic lands. The masses were historically more right in their feelings than the politicians were in their acts. None the less, war aims played a paramount part in public discussions. But again the problem was wrongly stated. Annexationists, advocates of a peace by victory, and admirers of the generals in command were all lumped together and placed in opposition to defeatists, advocates of a peace by understanding, and adherents of parliamentaryism. What was lacking was the politician who could drown the quarrel over war aims with the sound of his appeal to defend the nation. But he would have had first to break the omnipotence of the Army Command.

In an article which appeared in his paper, the *Deutsche Stimmen*, on July 25, 1919, Stresemann gave a final report on the chief circumstances of the war years. He levelled reproaches against Bethmann-Hollweg. He had been without initiative; he did not know how to win confidence; he had everywhere produced the impression that nothing went right with him, that ill luck dogged his path. Stresemann wrote: 'The Pan-Germanists have often been assailed with the reproach that if their policy had been carried out the whole world would have become hostile to Germany. Well, the undoubtedly anti-German policy of Bethmann did not leave many neutral States in the world.' The confusion is obvious. It was the decisions of the generals, it was above all the unrestricted U-boat warfare which brought America, which brought so many neutral States, into the enemy coalition. In Stresemann's account the realities of the situation are concealed. He takes what should have been laid on the shoulders of the generals and piles it on Bethmann's. Sentiment made him want the generals to be the saviours of their country, and so Bethmann must bear the load of their guilt. Sentiment, feeling is overpowering in him. Even in a letter written in 1927 to the Investigation Sub-Committee he says that it was the creation of the kingdom of Poland that brought the National Liberals into opposition to Bethmann. Here is the same instinctive prejudice, for the proclamation of the Polish State was a military measure. It was done at General von Beseler's instigation, and it would not have been done without the assent, the cordial assent, of Ludendorff.

In a report which Stresemann made after the July crisis he said that Erzberger's critical disquisition on the U-boat question was only a means to his end of the peace resolution, that his motives were mysterious and the change of attitude on the part of the Centrists inexplicable. But Erzberger's statement was undoubtedly clear enough, or it would not have made—and on Stresemann, too—the strong impression that it did make. Stresemann no longer wants to admit the truth. He says, 'There was no mention of panic in the Main Commission.' That is the most noteworthy sentence. It is not even tactical considerations that make him speak like that. He is simply holding fast to the old policy of sacrificing only the Chancellor, and has forgotten his own emotion under the arguments of Erzberger and the impressions of General Hoffman which Erzberger detailed. He could not hold on to hope, to confidence, if he regarded steadily the situation created by the Army Command. Therefore the memory of this 'aghastness' into which Erzberger's account had brought him must be wiped from the memory. It disappeared from his consciousness.

CHAPTER IV

THE HAMMER OF LUDENDORFF

STRESEMANN to himself and to others represented the military situation as brilliant. In formulating war-aims he was precise: 'The Army Command are our guarantee that Germany will receive the assurances she needs for the future.' Protests had come from party organizations throughout the country against a peace without annexations to which the National Liberal parliamentary party with reservations had adhered. He gave expression to the ideas of the protesters without committing himself. 'If we occupied Kurland, Esthonia, and Lithuania, and therewith possessed hegemony in the Baltic, in all the German lands, if our flag waved over Calais and so let us create a German Gibraltar on the Atlantic, who could make us give these up if we could hold out in the field?' That was romance triumphing, but a prosaic statement followed: 'But that is not the situation to-day.' No one in the party, 'if we could conclude a peace of dictation', would oppose the annexation of foreign territory because of its effects on the reconciliation of the peoples. On the other hand, a continuation of the war in order to make further annexations possible should be rejected. It is the same antithesis.

An able exposition which said much but left more unsaid. Erzberger's motives and his arguments were all mysterious. Why did he want the peace resolution? That was incomprehensible. Bethmann's fall was represented as the result of a series of diplomatic mistakes, many of which had been committed long before his time. Only the unfortunate relations with Italy and Roumania could be laid to his charge. The Army Command was treated as if it had nothing to do with the situation; its activities were not called in question. The article ended by quoting 'the splendid phrase' of Hindenburg: 'The times are difficult, but victory is certain.' If victory was certain, then all these troublesome reflections were unnecessary. A politician who was determined to be master of his craft had to cry out: 'Victory is not certain', as Erzberger did, in order then to make renunciation. Stresemann too made his renunciation. He renounced domination over the Reichstag. It is true that he declared that the parliamentary system should be accepted. But 'a parliamentary system in Germany could only be a German parliamentary system. For example, the German people would never understand or endure a civilian being made Minister of War or going to the Admiralty'. The supremacy of the soldiers is guaranteed for the future; in other words, the constitutional dualism, 'political activity and military activity', which means military supremacy. In parliamentary countries there was a civilian War Minister who controlled the commander-in-chief—if necessary, dismissed him. The words which Stresemann had uttered before the war crisis he did not utter again. When he gave his support to Erzberger, the Under-Secretary of State, Zimmermann, said to the deputy Haussmann: 'Do you know that Stresemann? . . .

I will not speak of him; the thing is a scandal. Now he is attacking us, and in December he was jubilating over a torpedoing because it would make war with America inevitable.' Then unbroken he had believed; now he felt it his duty to strengthen the belief of others.

At the time of his attack on Bethmann, Stresemann's candidate for the Chancellorship was Prince von Bülow, who, driven by war from his home in Rome, was holding a little political court in the Adlon Hotel. His nomination would have been significant. His authority was great enough to prevent him being simply a tool of the Army Command. The influence of the Reichstag on the fate of the Empire could only be secured by means of a man of will and personality. How would the inevitable conflict with the Army Command have ended? It would have had to come if Bülow appreciated the situation and was willing to turn will into deed.

The whole of the younger generation of parliamentarians, especially Erzberger and Richthofen, wanted Bülow in power. They had even won to his side the leaders of the parties. Bülow would have been the man, the only man, whom Stresemann would have followed even against the generals. The saying about personality, 'the one fortunate possession of the children of men', was to Stresemann not merely a phrase. He has often been reproached for change of purpose, vacillation of opinion. Such changes to him were all right where a thesis, a theory was concerned—he was a very Proteus in tactics—but not for his relation to men. He was loyal wherever he once honoured or admired. There was really no excuse for letting Bethmann fall, unless a better man was ready to take his place. Michaelis's nomination followed so swiftly on the heels of Bethmann's dismissal that the idea of Bülow as Chancellor never got a chance. Prince Max of Baden declares: 'Parliament showed the will to power; it rattled the sabre; it provoked the most difficult political crisis since the founding of the Empire and counted on it as a certainty that a solution would be found from above', and 'Reactionary circles exulted that a Chancellor was presented to the Reichstag majority who was not its man of confidence but actually its man of no-confidence.' Lieut.-Col. von Haeften wrote on July 31st in a letter to Prince Max: 'I feared that at the important, perhaps the most immediately important task, the elimination of the Social Democratic Party as a decisive factor in home as in foreign politics Herr Michaelis would scarcely succeed.' When Michaelis sought to strengthen his position with the sensation of the alleged mutiny in the fleet it only became untenable. Stresemann mocked at 'the few in our party who maintained the obsolete view that every chancellor or secretary of state must be applauded the moment he begins to speak against the Social Democrats'.

In the 'Inter-Party Commission' Social Democrats, Progressives, and Centrists—the parties of the July resolution—worked together; the 'cynical lobbies' called the Commission a 'soviet'. The National Liberals sometimes belonged to it, sometimes did not. Now they entered it again. On October 23rd, deputies, with Stresemann at their head, handed to Valentini, the head of the Emperor's Civil Cabinet, a document which treated a change in the chancellorship as something already agreed upon, and requested the Emperor to see to it that the new Chancellor before his official nomination should come to an understanding with the parties. By express resolution of the Commission the document mentioned no names. To Kühlmann, Richthofen made an attempt on behalf of Bülow. Stresemann found a way which promised better. He got into touch with Duke Ernst Gunther of Schleswig-Holstein, the brother of the Empress. All was in vain. The Emperor would not have Bülow, who had failed to protect him in 1908 at the time of the *Daily Telegraph* affair, the 'beast', as he called him then. He may have feared that Bülow 'had his cabinet all ready made. Then apparently I would not have been consulted further'. And the Army Command had no wish for a Chancellor who might be expected to show independence.

To Michaelis succeeded Count Hertling. With him came what people then called 'parliamentarization'. Stresemann gave free expression to the disillusion which the refusal to accept his candidate had been. 'How strongly personal considerations can prevail over serious interests,' he wrote in the *Nationalzeitung*, 'is seen in Germany's case in the shameful way in which one of her ablest political and diplomatic minds is allowed to waste itself unused in the world war.' These must have been 'mean motives' that prevented Bülow's return to the Chancellorship. Also to make no use of him at the eventual world peace conference 'would be a challenge to public opinion which one hopes will not be made at that crisis'. Stresemann was a monarchist, it is true; but he was no Byzantine.

By that sentence it is clearly seen that, however strong was his feeling for the honour of the Imperial House, it did not prevent him from publicly blaming his sovereign. From all over the country came National Liberal voices against the maintenance by the Chancellor of the peace resolution and against democratization, and accusations that the Reichstag had encroached on the Crown's right of nomination. Stresemann defended himself. The only care of the protesters had been to preserve that tranquillity which would prevent internal disunions disturbing the generals at their task of winning the war for the Fatherland. He added praise for Michaelis for his famous reservation to the peace resolution, 'as I conceive it'. So he avoided committing himself too far in view of coming peace negotiations.

Hertling was a Catholic Conservative. As a result of years of absence, the former leader of the Centrists had become a stranger to the Reichstag. As a Bavarian, and by birth a Hessian, he did not seem a suitable person to carry through electoral reform in Prussia. The introduction of the Parliamentary system was expected of him; to that introduction he was opposed. In recent days Erzberger had become the decisive influence in the Centrum. Hertling was his enemy. He was seventy-four, and the infirmities of age compelled him to stop all work after eight o'clock at night. His eyelids used to close in the midst of a parliamentary storm. His eyes were already so weak that reading was painful. Almost everything spoke against his nomination. The parliamentary leaders, including Stresemann, did not want him. Kühlmann intervened and showed the majority parties that here at last was the long-hoped-for chance to make the cabinet at least partially a Parliamentary one. If this chance failed, then it was greatly to be feared that the partisans of a dictatorship, the enemies of the Reichstag, would get the upper hand. It was agreed that the Württemberg Progressive, Payer—and equally a man trusted by the Social Democrats—should be Vice-Chancellor, and the National Liberal Friedberg, Vice-President of the Prussian Ministry. Friedberg, fundamentally a Conservative, though at the moment in favour of electoral reform, was nominated without more ado. Payer's appointment was secured only with difficulty against Hertling's wishes. The Chief of the Civil Cabinet, Valentini, declared that 'all this parliamentaryism was only a farce which would last but a few months'. The ideas of the Army Command were, as the deputy Martin Spahn happily expressed them, 'God, let the Reichstag win a little more influence, may they quietly win even a little official influence, which anyway they possess in practice already; we will bubble them afterwards. What needs to be done at the front, will then be done, as far as the people are concerned, under cover of their responsibility.'

In the conversations which took place before the new ministers were confirmed in office, Friedberg had himself proposed to Stresemann to resign the Prussian Vice-Presidency in his favour. Stresemann had refused. The position of Vice-President was no longer a decisive one; it had no concern with the most important decisions of policy. The Constitution, whose text had never been altered, had actually fundamentally changed on this point. The Bundesrat was no longer the real government of the Empire.

There was a war cabinet, the Imperial Chancellor with the Secretaries of State. But the war cabinet, too, was impotent. Its most prominent Parliamentary member, Friedrich von Payer, was sixty years old. From the date of his nomination until February he was ill and out of touch. In the summer of 1918 Hertling spent months at Spa with the Army Command, and Payer, who had to represent the Cabinet in Parliament, never for the most part knew what was being decided. The function of the Prussian Vice-President was to carry through electoral reform in that State. But reform made no progress up to the date when the Revolution took up the task and finished it. Meantime foreign policy was conducted independently by the Secretary of State, von Kühlmann, that is, independently of the Chancellor and the Reichstag, 'in agreement with the Army Command', which, against all constitutional practice, caused the peace of Brest to be countersigned by General Hoffman. When the agreement broke down, it was all up with Kühlmann. The debates in the Prussian Parliament were of secondary importance; they too could only serve 'by leaving Hindenburg and Ludendorff to conquer in peace'. Stresemann, in order to become a member of the Bundesrat, would have to give up his seat in the Reichstag. His position as leader of a Parliamentary party seemed to him a more important one.

The majority Parties—the Parties of the peace resolution—lay low and shammed death in the period of Hertling's chancellorship. It was not because they had men whom they could trust in the ministry, not simply because of Hertling's parliamentary and diplomatic cleverness. The events on the fronts had a stronger influence. The collapse of Russia, the defeat of Roumania, the conclusion of peace treaties in the East, the spring offensive in the West—in comparison with such events, of the preparation for which none of the civilian ministers knew anything, the increasing distress of the nation, the formidable strike movement of January 1918 took second place. The declaration which Erzberger in July 1917 had made in the Main Commission was toned down. He himself was now busied more with founding kingdoms and assigning crowns than with the attempt to comprehend the military situation. In the East there were a million troops—later indeed only half that number—who were lost for the West, and the war was lost by their absence. The politician who, as in duty bound, saw farther than the generals, should have seen to the liquidation of the Russian adventure. The need to embark upon it was well enough founded in the need for providing foodstuffs. Later even the soldiers had to agree that smuggling would have procured just the same quantities. The influence which once the Reichstag seemed to have won, disappeared. When at a Crown Council at Spa on July 14th, it was resolved to make peace because defeat could no longer be avoided, the Vice-Chancellor, Payer, was not present. It was not considered necessary to invite him to attend.

In these days Stresemann's imperialism rose high. He spoke and wrote in terms which once he would have been very far from using. An unusual acerbity against political opponents crept in. The belief in victory became an article of faith which if any man should gainsay he was guilty of sin. When he

STRESEMANN AS AN ORATOR

THREE CHARACTERISTIC ATTITUDES

pictured to himself the aims, the victories, of the war, romance triumphed and practical sense hid its face.

Stresemann was not one who failed to understand those who differed from him ; one would seek in vain in the writings and speeches of many years for what is called provocation. In 1918, however, a strain of nervousness creeps into his writing. He speaks of 'Herr Sobelson, called Radek, who is careful to write under the name Parabellum and who belongs to the Spartacus group'. Of the strikes he declares that 'all these movements have been directly instigated by the Entente'. It is quite unusual to find him indulging in that abuse of the Socialists so common among the Pan-Germanists. Now things are different. 'The Social Democrats have participated in preparing these strikes, and they must take the responsibility for them. The strikes they plotted are nothing else than high treason to the State.' In the Austrian munition factories the first strikes had broken out. At once he launches a diatribe against 'the Social Democratic Party of Austria, composed in the main of non-Germans, and the public saturated with democracy and cosmopolitanism which reads the *Neue Freie Presse*, the *Zeit*, the *Neues Wiener Tageblatt*, and other rags of the same kidney'. As without, so within. 'Too long it has been the custom to cite the press of the capital as if it were the authentic voice of Germany. The *Berliner Tageblatt* gives no true idea of what Germany is thinking.'

As in this repudiation, so in his positive aims. Scheidemann had said that whoever believed in victory was a fool. 'The fool who believes in victory will, please God, hold fast in the West.

6

Then we will renew ourselves and, uninfluenced by the July resolution, place ourselves before the issue —how we shall find security against those who in this world war have shown themselves the deadly enemies of Germany.' That, even counting all his earlier reservations, was a denial of his own past. Stresemann too had taken sides with the 'July opinion'. A glance at the map was enough to show any man of sense that the Baltic lands could not afford 'security', but only made the defence of the Empire more difficult. Stresemann could not have failed to see that. But considerations of honour are now decisive for him. 'We shall march because the threatened massacre of our Baltic kin calls us.' No annexations, however. But that was mere playing with words. 'A free Baltic State in close relations with Germany under our military, political, spiritual, and cultural protection, I think it would be one of the fairest aims of this world war if we so protected that true piece of Germany, so intimately fused it with Germany as it itself desires.' And in the West: 'It is the height of folly to think that the German working class will embark on a campaign of sharp resistance to the German State if, after the peace, the French minefields belong to Germany and an independent Flanders comes under Germany's aegis.' 'Russia, reft of its border peoples will see over against it a great Bulgaria whose frontier in the Dobrudja will stretch to the Danube.'

In April Stresemann spoke in Hamburg. A frenzy had seized him. 'As the Lord God lets the storm sweep over the sea, so will the sword, the bride of the storm, sweep down when we move to attack. That it is possible for the enemy to make our victory uncertain, no one in the enemy countries, no one in the really neutral countries believes, and it is only sad that the doubt that we shall conquer finds all too much expression in Germany.' And a week later: 'What is happening on the Western front and what is preparing so far surpasses the power of man to picture that words no longer can keep pace with events.' Always in speeches, in articles, recurs a quotation from Conrad Ferdinand Meyer's 'Ulrich von Hutten':

> All my regret is for the hour
> I was not in the field,
> All my regret is for the day
> My arms I did not wield,
> All my regret—upon my head
> Repentant ashes lie
> Because I did not stouter hold
> That victory was nigh.

Stresemann knew literature well; he loved fine poetry; he gladly joyed to find his own thoughts expressed in it. But this verse is more than mere interpretation. Does it refer only to others? Or to him who quotes it? Does it refer to the staggering blow of humiliation when Erzberger in 1917 pictured the military situation, as General Hoffman saw it? Does it refer to the often-repeated saying that the war was lost diplomatically before it began in the field? Does it refer to the doubts which, even at this time of severest crisis, dwelt in his breast and made his heart uneasy? In his diary General Hoffman notes: 'I laughed over Stresemann's flaming speech of protest. I often think of his meeting with Bernstorff at Witting's and his bearing then. And now he is a fanatical Pan-German, militarist and annexationist!' Witting, who was the brother of Maximilian Harden, was formerly Burgomaster of Posen and director of the Darmstädter Bank, and had become a Radical pacifist during the war.

In a communication to the Investigation Sub-Committee of the Reichstag in 1927 Stresemann said: 'That by the failure of the offensive in March and May, the hope of a German victory finally disappeared, was never admitted to me by the soldiers although Colonel Bauer repeatedly deprecated too great confidence on the part of public opinion. Any warning from the Army Command that we must make sacrifices in order to obtain peace did not arrive until September 30th. A very pessimistic impression of the general situation was given me at that time by Count Harry Kessler, who also asked me if we could bring ourselves to give up those portions of Alsace-Lorraine of which the French were then in occupation. This was a matter which I certainly thought could be discussed if there was any real prospect of making peace. The whole difficulty of the situation was clear to me from the latter half of June and that as a result of the information given me in Rügen by Baron von Maltzan, who gave me the impressions which he himself had gathered at the front.' Stresemann added that after the collapse of Russia—the collapse of Russia which happened at the turn of the year 1917–18!—he had up to October 1st thought that Germany was unconquerable, militarily speaking.

That communication is full of contradictions. The tension and uncertainty of these days is reflected in it. Any one who realized 'all the difficulty of the situation ' at the front as it existed in June 1918, could no longer hold that Germany could not be conquered. The almost unlimited air forces that the Allies possessed, their superiority in tanks, the small number of Germany's mobile divisions, the increasing dissolution of units, the falling strength of the battalions, the lack of horses in the artillery, the failing reserves, the desertions which steadily increased—any one who visited the front or the staffs and kept his ears and eyes open, any one who was not completely under the influence of a fixed idea, must have known how things stood and how badly they stood. He must also have known of the Entente's counter-attack on July 18th and of the black day of August 8th. Any one who had anything to do with formations at home or with the reserves must have had at least an inkling of the truth. The events which occurred when troops were being sent to the front were for Prussian officers scandalous and unparalleled; lack of discipline, direct disobedience had to be overlooked because there was no power to enforce either. These things it was not difficult to learn: everywhere Reserve and Landwehr officers had lost control. They would not, out of patriotic conviction, have concealed the facts from the National Liberal leader.

Only a miracle could prevent the end. But any one who believes, and wants to believe, will also firmly believe in a miracle. It was shortly after he had received his information from Baron von Maltzan that Stresemann sharply criticized the fallen Kühlmann because he ' allowed public opinion to think of peace as if our military successes were not so great that in them alone lay the possibility of peace '. 'Not the speeches of the statesmen, not the negotiations of diplomatists, nor diplomatic notes, nor Reichstag resolutions, but, as Lloyd George has said, only the hammer of Ludendorff, the strength of our soldiers, the strength of our armed might.' And again: 'Never could we have had less reason to doubt of victory than now.' Lichnowsky, and with him diplomacy, was damned. Wilson's League of Nations was rejected. 'Real security for our political and economic future' was demanded. It was already August when Stresemann's polemic rose to its fiercest intensity. Hans Delbrück, in the *Preussische Jahrbücher*, had criticized Kühlmann's successor, the Secretary of State, Hinze, because he was not spiking the guns of the Pan-Germanists. Stresemann angrily asked: 'How many years' imprisonment would Herr Professor Delbrück have got, had he published his article in New York or Paris?'

Later Stresemann explained much of what he had said by pleading tactical necessity. Kühlmann had to go because in the hour when Germany was engaged in the decisive battle, he allowed himself to express doubts of victory. There was only one course, 'Keep on firing.' But later explanations are dubious; standpoint and viewpoint have alike altered; the speaker no longer recognizes himself. The unusual tone, the accumulation of invective, the wounding words, all show his own inner soreness and perplexity. It is the repetition of earlier events. Excess of feeling conquers the politician. The most obvious thing for the greatness of the Fatherland is victory in the field; victory is incarnated in Ludendorff, and the more doubt presses upon him, the more violently is he drawn into the unknown;

the more freely, more plainly, belief in a miracle overcomes his reason. Even when he speaks of things of which there is no longer any doubt—it is now the end of August—of ' the first million Americans ', of the ineffectiveness of the U-boat campaign, Stresemann calls for ' the strong faith of optimism ' and calls what has been attained, the conquest of the East, ' the bases of Germany's future '. Seven years, eight years, eleven years later, after the nation has gone down into the deepest abyss of misery, and there is no more heard of bringing home the sheaves—conquests, countries, coasts, minefields—but only of tiny alleviations of an almost intolerable situation, of pale glimmers of hope of a safe future, many a time the same faith in destiny comes from him, expressed in the same words. But what then was to be solid, attainable, real, was later unsubstantial, an aery romantic pageant.

The idea of gains in the East occurs again in the report to the Investigation Sub-Committee. Stresemann, even in 1927, thought that a stand could have been made on the Meuse and the Eastern conquests saved. Then the life would have been squeezed out of France by the occupation. The passage of the Rhine he held to be militarily impossible. Here is the same contradiction. If there had been a retreat to the Rhine, no French territory would have been occupied. And at the Armistice there stood on the Western front, where otherwise the respective strengths were about equal, two million young Americans. Here the thinking process has degenerated into pure irrationality.

CHAPTER V

THE TWILIGHT OF THE GODS

ON October 1, 1918, Major von dem Bussche by order of the Army Command addressed the party leaders: 'The resolution must be taken to regard the further prosecution of the war as useless. Every twenty-four hours the situation becomes worse and allows the enemy to recognize our real weakness.' All his hearers were dismayed. But an eye-witness tells us that the deputy Stresemann looked 'as if something had fallen upon him'.

Already, on September 26th, Bulgaria had asked for an armistice. At the end of August, Payer had spent a day arguing with Ludendorff to try to extort the renunciation of Belgium. That nothing of grotesqueness should be lacking the General Quartermaster insisted in the formula in which final agreement was reached on a reservation about the Flemings.

Through Major von dem Bussche, Ludendorff let it be known that the Reichstag had now to take over power. The Reichstag had no candidates for office. An outsider in politics—people knew nothing of him save as the author of a couple of mild and elegant speeches—Prince Max of Baden, became Chancellor. His cabinet was the first Imperial Government in the true sense of the words. The Secretaries of State were responsible ministers. In the weeks that followed the feeling of the actors in every circumstance was 'too late'. Prince Max wrote to his cousin, the Grand Duke of Baden: 'I thought I should arrive five minutes before the hour; I arrived five minutes after it.'

Many thought of a concentration cabinet from Westarp as far left as possible. But already, on September 30th, Haussmann had said in the Inter-Party Commission, 'We need not burden ourselves with Stresemann.' The Chancellor-designate desired to base his government solidly on the majority Parties. At the reception of deputies he said to Stresemann that he needed him and his Party comrades not in the government but in opposition. Prince Max notes: 'Stresemann was astounded.' The National Liberals had left the Inter-Party Commission, the 'soviet', after the January strikes. Now they were in it again. Of their party the Secretary of State for Justice, Dr. von Krause, remained in the cabinet and Friedberg in the Prussian ministry, as did the Secretary of State for Food, von Waldow, a Conservative. But they played no part; they acted merely as observers for their Parties. The Reichstag had for long been accustomed not to follow a political leader. The evil custom which has completely distorted the parliamentary system in Germany made its first appearance; the parliamentary parties arranged who should join the government.

The generals used their dictatorial power for the last time; they compelled the Government to send a demand for an armistice and to accept the armistice conditions. That was a matter on which the soldiers had clearly to advise more than in any of the political questions in which in the past years they had decided as a sovereign from whose decision there is no appeal. But this time the resistance was stouter than ever it had been before. Prince Max did not wish to end hostilities so abruptly. The democratic Secretary of State, Haussmann, drew up a proclamation for the prosecution of the war. The Conservative Parliamentary Party, Admiral von Tirpitz, the President of the Prussian Upper House, Count Arnim-Boitzenburg, protested. Heads of schools, officials, members of the learned professions, bombarded the Chancellor with letters and telegrams. The journalist Georg Bernhard, the poet Richard Dehmel, the banker Max Warburg, did all they possibly could to prevent the war ending as it did. Walter Rathenau appealed publicly for a *levée en masse*. He addressed to the Minister of War, Scheuch, a comprehensive memorandum showing on how many soldiers he could reckon and how the national defence could be organized. The Chancellor's own feelings were entirely with those who wanted to fight on until the armistice conditions were altered. Stresemann demanded that 'the verbal and written statements of the Army leaders and of their chiefs of staff on the present military situation should be produced'. For him the military authority was still unshaken. The soldiers and the Army Command decided—for the armistice.

In the articles which Stresemann wrote in these weeks and in a great Reichstag speech, there is plain the revolution which events have brought about in himself. If any one seeks to understand how a man becomes a statesman through mistakes and prejudices, through disillusionment and bitter experience, through self-conquest, above all things, through control of the feelings that fill his heart to overflowing, he should study what Stresemann wrote and said after he had lived through this shattering blow. There will come a time when he seems to return to that blindness to which he had clung, and again a time when what now troubles him will serve to raise him again and advantage the nation. A man might be born with the vision of Cassandra, with the political sense of Aristotle, and the clear-sightedness of a Hebrew prophet, yet he would not be a statesman but only the counsellor of a statesman. What makes the national leader, the leader of a democracy, is excess of feeling, and he matures to knowledge through painful renunciations. It is no suitable recommendation for the politician that he has known and prophesied everything beforehand.

'We have had to learn by experience in this world war that the parliamentary system creates close bonds and connexions between people, government, and State such as I in peace time would not have believed possible of a time when war was shattering the State's very foundations.'

'If ever a Bismarck had had at his disposal a great and powerful workers' party which had consented to enter the government and take upon itself responsibility for the State, he would have been the first to have used their strength to serve his own purposes.'

'We have drawn the conclusion from what was developed and from what we experienced in these years of war of development in home and foreign affairs, that the system which had led us so far had justified its right to continued existence.'

Stresemann must also say something which will

exonerate himself and his party. He points out—and can rightly point out—that he never regarded the war as lost 'if we did not attain this or that war-aim, but that, as soon as it came to a question of peace, we should place ourselves behind the Army Command and the political leaders if they were united on war-aims'. In any case, behind the Army Command.

To the student Stresemann the National Liberals were too governmental. The political candidate injected desire for power into their leaders. Then had come the swift rise in the party, the friendship of Bassermann, the succession to him—and he himself has become governmental. He had never—that is certain—terrorized the government over Kurland and Flanders the way the Pan-Germanists did, although he too was enthusiastic for far-off lands. He had in that, too, been governmental; at the very most he had only been a genial, a most considerate opponent. But that is past. What he now says about 'standing behind the Army Command', or when he speaks of 'explanations of our responsible positions'—that belongs to the past. From the terrible disillusionment when he saw his gods destroyed he matured to will to power.

'There is a contradiction which also is expressed in the question—parliamentary system or German system? In our earlier days high officialdom and the people were two things between which there was no link. When in England the workers did not wish to go on working, which meant a fall in the output of munitions, then the Minister of Labour went down to the miners, spoke to them, roused them, and when they saw the Minister as a man before them, since he stood up to them as man to man and asked their confidence, then quite different methods were possible there than could be used here, where, if it is desired to influence the people, the *Norddeutsche Allgemeine Zeitung* is used.'

Only a very short time before, the Secretary of State, Wallraf, had refused to receive representatives of the striking workers, and Stresemann had stoutly defended him when he was attacked because of his refusal. The Social Democrats, even the Majority Socialists who had got the strikers back into the factories again, he declared equally guilty of high treason to the Fatherland. A politician must learn. In storm and with agony he learns.

He is still farther from his earlier path when he comes to the military domain. A certain sense of loyalty makes him call it the 'military-technical domain'. He indicates the Ministry of War, but does not name it. But he hits at the all-powerful Army Command and every one knows what he means

'The Minister of Munitions, Lloyd George, did more for England than Germany got before the Hindenburg programme. The construction of submarines was neglected, and many other mistakes were made for which we shall have to pay, perhaps with much of the future of our Fatherland.'

'But our system of its own accord rejected that part of our education, the technical, from which it could have drawn its most powerful support in the military domain. That we had to learn technique from amateurs in military craftsmanship in England and America, was an unparalleled disillusion for those who had believed that, if we had had to pay with loss of freedom, at least we were in this domain the great teachers of the world, having reached a standard that others could not attain. Then we had a bitter experience when we were called together to prepare our auxiliary services law. When we asked in horror how it could be that our munitions output had declined at a time when England was increasing hers seventeenfold, the representative of the army told us: "Aye, but you see we had no Lloyd George to organize things in Germany, as Lloyd George did in England." '

'When one realizes that, from the autumn of 1914, the German authorities had been offered tanks by German industry, when we see that the competent authorities in German industry were never used in connexion with U-boat construction, then one feels very bitter over the opportunities that were lost.'

'It was the system established by the Ministry of War that we have to thank for swindling and profiteering.'

He quotes the words which the Secretary of State for the Navy, Admiral von Capelle, had used in the Main Commission of the Reichstag: 'The military aid America can give is nil, simply nil, simply nil.' And finally he attacks directly the methods of deception used by the bemazed Army Command: 'The expressions used by the Wolff Agency reports about the exhaustion of Foch's reserves in spring were also completely exaggerated.'

On October 13th the local presidents and general secretaries of the party were summoned to Berlin. Then the impression made by Major von dem Bussche's revelation was still fresh. Stresemann made his report: 'Collapse of moral at Headquarters; the Army Command throws up the sponge.' The rolling of thunder over the fallen gods.

'One question must be asked—whether it is possible still to defend the system which in that very department, the military-technical, in which it should have found its greatest support, let itself be found inferior to nations which placed amateurs in that branch at the War Ministry.'

Now he no longer repented 'that he had not stouter held that victory was certain'. Now he no longer felt that Germany could never abide a civilian as War Minister. Now he repented that he had not made himself Minister of War, that he had not himself organized the munitions output, that he had not himself gone to address the strikers. He had learned to mistrust others, to mistrust all which he had not himself seen and handled, to mistrust the experts, the pontifical idols to which Germany had always bowed down. Aghast, he had been once; once it had been 'as if something had fallen on him'. The appalling disillusion now at last found full expression. He had trusted, and what he trusted had failed him. In the years which follow we will often find him in opposition, in secret or open opposition, so long as he does not rule himself until he does rule himself. We will see him during all these years fight untiringly for power. The certainty that one day he would be summoned to it was born in these hours when he lay abased in the dark abyss of disillusionment.

Stresemann was no longer in the main stream of events. On November 9th he went with the other representatives of the bourgeois parties to the Imperial Chancellery and sent in to announce his arrival to Prince Max of Baden. No one knows what the deputies wanted there. It is even unknown whether the Prince ever was told that visitors had called. In his memoirs he gives a detailed account of what happened that day, but there is not a word about the visit of the deputies. Nor do Scheidemann, Haussmann, or Payer, who were all there or thereabouts, tell us anything. The sting of that wasted visit still remained with Stresemann long after. He wrote on November 9, 1919: 'Prince Max of Baden wanted neither to speak to nor to see the representatives of the three bourgeois parties. We stood in the great hall and patiently waited for something to happen.'

The event is only of symbolic significance. After the endless nerve-racking negotiations with Imperial Head-quarters over the question of abdication which the Emperor stubbornly refused, Prince Max had only one care—whether Ebert and his party would be able to save Germany from Bolshevism. Loyalists, officers, bourgeois were now of so little importance that they no longer existed.

Then came a new blow which had more important consequences. After the Revolution all the middle-class parties sought new mottoes, new content, new men, new names. In face of the high tide of Socialism, there seemed only one aim—the prevention of Socialism in practice. Socialism or not—that seemed the one problem. The Majority Socialists wanted a National Assembly. Thus parliamentary democracy was saved. No one wished to go further to the right than that.

In place of the Conservative Party appeared the German National People's Party. The Centrists, now appearing as the Christian People's Party, wished to attract members of all confessions. The National Liberals were to unite with the Progressives. Everything was ready on November 15th, but the fusion was celebrated simultaneously with its failure.

New men had appeared meantime, a picked body of them, Rathenau, Gerhart Hauptmann, Richard Dehmel, Albert Einstein, Bernstorff, Alfred Weber, not to speak of Stinnes, Stegewald, and Sombart, who were recruiting for a Democratic People's League. A section of the National Liberals went with them, not just a few from the left wing of the party, but men too from the centre and the right. Privy Councillor Friedberg, one of the most conservative of all the National Liberals, their leader in the three class franchise fight, had at first taken part in the attempt at fusion, then was present at the conversations with the Democrats, went off annoyed with Stresemann, and ended in the Democratic Party. The confusion sometimes could hardly be more confounded.

In the foundation group of the Democrats, gentlemen of the Press, Theodor Wolff and Martin Carbe of the *Berliner Tageblatt*, Arthur Feiler of the *Frankfurter Zeitung*, Hellmut von Gerlach, Nuschke, editor-in-chief of the *Berliner Volkszeitung*, took over the leadership. The Left Press during the war had for the most part never seen eye to eye with Stresemann, and had shown its disapproval of him. Hence arose intimate enmities. Stresemann was on the point of proclaiming the united Liberal Party under an improvised name in order to create a *fait accompli*. He had no confidence in the friendliness of the new arrivals. But he let himself be restrained. Too many great names out of the old parties had come to the new one.

In the conference which finally met, the word, though unspoken, prevailed which in October Haussmann had used in the Inter-Party Commission: 'Now we need not burden ourselves with Stresemann.' He had been 'Ludendorff's young man'. What was wanted now was something quite different from what had ever been before—the League of Nations, the abandonment of the policy of force, an international regime of right and justice.

There was an easy way of showing that the old ways had been abandoned; the men who had up to then been leaders should retire into the background. But Stresemann felt that his whole political life was at stake. Bitterly he declared: 'The brutality with which negotiations were carried on by Professor Weber could hardly be surpassed.' He was beside himself with rage when he declared: 'They boasted of establishing a new ethic, and they wished first to establish who was worthy to co-operate in the new party'—two sentences closely related which say two very different things. The new ethic which Alfred Weber meant is in the policy which Stresemann was later to carry out. At the moment he believed that he heard doubts whether his own ethic was quite pure enough, and he objected that there were others 'quite as badly branded with vacillation and change of opinion as the parliamentarians, who were now described as the pillars of the old regime and whom it was desired to set aside'.

At the beginning of the war Erzberger had been one of Thyssen's directors and had elaborated a grandiose scheme of annexations. Georg Bernhard had been a protagonist of unrestricted U-boat warfare. Scheidemann had uttered the dangerous saying about 'the illusion that after this war any frontier will remain unaltered', a phrase on which, as his opponents of the left said, the war-aims of the Fatherland Party could quite well have been founded. Naturally many of the left were not quite free from an imperialist past. But that did not enter into it. No one wished a heresy hunt against repentant sinners. It all turned on trifles. And especially on what ideas were held by the outside public. To public opinion Stresemann was 'Ludendorff's young man'. That was an obvious reason why his name should not be attached to a pacifist programme, to a programme of international uprightness.

Stresemann simply did not understand that part of the argument. He held what had been done to him to be presumption as well as injustice. But as far as the politician is concerned, comprehension did not matter, nor did repentance nor insight nor the true line of development. His *métier* is not to withdraw into himself but to come out of—himself. He must carry himself through. He must carry himself through before he can carry through a programme. The will to power decides whether he will turn into a statesman. The impetus to publicity, to activity, then to set on the world the stamp of his own personality, was stronger than anything else in Stresemann. Here the true politician is revealed. He had suffered the most terrible reverses; the last failure, although it was a series of pinpricks rather than a blow, was perhaps all the more painful in its effects because of that. It needs only one drop to make the full glass run over. The refusal of the Democrats could be that drop in his case. Later Alfred Weber, who had opposed him 'with an unsurpassable brutality', gave him his most valued distinction, the Heidelberg doctorate. But at the moment the man he had outlawed nearly succumbed. Everything was a sham and a lie; the great aims of life had fallen in ruins; the base of his whole existence, the Party, had trampled him underfoot.

A week later appeared the manifesto of the German People's Party. Privy Councillor Friedberg, the Conservative, was to the left of it among the Democrats. He had declared to Stresemann: 'There is no money in the party chest, the rich subscribers have all gone to the new party.' But Stresemann's genius for discovery found other sources of revenue. So many people had gathered money during the war. A portion of it might be placed at the service of good political aims, even if it came from less worthy sources than the old revenues of the National Liberals. Stresemann had been overthrown; he had submitted, lay prostrate. But only for a moment. He turned his back on the responsibilities of which others had deprived him.

Stresemann had risen high in the Reichstag and in the Party. If as long as Bassermann lived he was, because of his confidential relations with him, really the leader of the Party, after Bassermann's death on July 28, 1917, he was its official leader. He had not won leadership without a struggle, without difficulty. Influential members of the Party had wanted to make Schiffer leader. When Stresemann heard of it he was hard put to it. But Schiffer had been ready to take part in Bethmann's intrigue against Bassermann. Besides Stresemann's name by his public work, his speeches up and down the country had become known everywhere. That decided the issue in his favour. Now even his position as party-leader had gone. He contented himself with second place. Heinze was president. If he could but feel firm ground beneath him once again . . .

The failure of the negotiations with the Progressives and the Democrats gave Stresemann to a very great extent freedom and independence. The programme of the People's Party—it was at first to be called the National Democratic People's Party—was liberal. In it was demanded complete reform of the Foreign Office—as is known a favourite subject with Stresemann—then a national army, equal suffrage, right of coalition. A programme of yesterday. But no liberal demands could be put forward which went farther than the circumstances of the hour permitted. There was no recognition of the Republic. All else was left to the imagination. Voters for the party could only be men and women who were not content with the new regime and were afraid of what was to come. It entered the National Assembly two and twenty strong, the smallest of the parties. The smallness of the party was due less to the small number of discontented and the anxious, than to lack of time and money. As far as agitation in the country was concerned, Stresemann had done all he could. Often conditions were little encouraging. In Nordhorn his meeting was broken up and he was struck on the head, had to flee and spend the night in a cellar. He was fired at in Westphalia. At the time he hardly ever alluded to these two experiences. The associations throughout the land had for the most part gone over to the Democrats. That party offered defence against socialization. The fear of the Socialists swamping all the other parties made everything else of no account. Stresemann wrote at the time, 'Why is there all this division?' There could only be one programme for a middle-class party. So completely had the middle-classes been forced on to the defensive.

After the vicissitudes of the negotiations between National Liberals, Progressives, and Democrats, it might have been thought that the two parties would stand by one another in Parliament. But the sharp division between 'the two Germanys' existed between them too. The position in the National Assembly for the People's Party as a result of the election was this. To the right of them were no more than forty-four Nationalists; to the left, huge parties, the Social Democrats with one hundred and thirty-six members, the Centrists with ninety-one, the Democrats with seventy-five. And on the extreme left were twenty-two Independent Socialists. Such a situation counted for more than good intentions. Even if the two and twenty had sought with the best will in the world to be a centre party, they could not have escaped being a party of the right.

So it was only natural that their appeal should be directed to people whose sympathies were right and who needed to be united and represented. The idea of union with the Nationalists was earnestly discussed. From that time to the present the two parties form but one party in the Prussian Chamber. The attitude of the party was not simply negative. It worked with the Nationalists—a mere attitude of nothing but refusal would have been contrary to the character of the party and especially to the character of Stresemann, who was ever seeking a chance to work and, at least, a chance to co-operate. In the handbook of the National Liberals he had placed under the rubric, 'Aim in Life'—'work at the roaring loom of time.' But in the actual circumstances all that the party could do was to recognize the limits of the possible. It goes without saying that the party rejected the Peace Treaty and the Constitution.

In Berlin one of its election placards read, 'Only the German People's Party can free you from the red fetters.' For the motto Stresemann later disclaimed all responsibility.

Prince Max of Baden's action in handing over the conduct of affairs to Ebert, Stresemann called 'disgraceful treachery'; the change in the German colours 'shameless abandonment of everything that is noble'. He declared: 'Truly it will be disgraceful if a majority for the change be found in a Parliament calling itself German.'

He attacked bitterly his former leader in politics, Naumann, because he said that the monarchy 'in the great purgatory of the world had not given any proof of ability'. How had things gone on so shortly before that? Stresemann passed judgement when he said: 'The system which has hitherto led us has proved its right to continued existence.' If one likes one can make the difference clear. It lies in the difference between the words 'monarchy' and 'system'. But what mattered was the great gulf between them.

Then Stresemann made his appeal—and the party conference at Jena applauded him: 'To live and to dream in Germany's past is the best which is left for us to do in the Sabbath hours of life.'

An idea, better called a fantasy, became his favourite theme, a beacon to his followers: 'We could have gone on fighting.'

'We had our Hannibal. . . . We stood before Paris as Hannibal before Rome. But just as in those old days the Roman sense of the State won a victory over the Carthaginian lack of it . . .'

'Had but one hundred thousand men, a nucleus, stood firm, we could have gone to the peace conference with a pen in one hand and a sword in the other.'

'If all the deserters from the front had melted away and only a tiny army had remained in the lines, fallen back fighting to the Meuse and, if it had to be, withdrawn to the German frontier . . .' All that has nothing to do with the realities of the military situation. It would be useless to set forth why such a plan could not have been seriously discussed any more than Rathenau's great conception of a national resistance which found none to hear it and believe.

There were no practical considerations either, nothing at all practical, about his cry, 'Wälse, Wälse, where is thy sword?' That was a romantic wail that rose from the heart and went to the hearts of others. It was also self-accusation. Had he not been once 'aghast' when Erzberger detailed the sad prophecies of General Hoffman? What did he do when the information brought by Baron von Maltzan had made the seriousness of the situation clear to him? When Major von dem Bussche made his report, was it not the deputy Stresemann who seemed 'as if something had fallen on him'? When Rathenau outlined his plan for resistance, did he not content himself with the memoranda of the army leaders? In secret his own mistakes, his own failure, worked in his mind and made his accusations against others ever sharper, ever more bitter. The plainer the bitterness, the less is the reminder heard: You could have done what Lloyd George and Clemenceau did—these two always appear in Stresemann's speeches as heroes, as saviours of their countries—you could like them have seized power from the generals, taken up the battle in their stead, won a better peace. From the events of the past, confused and full of fantasies, comes the synthesis: 'The sword of the Volsung—we broke it ourselves in the shameful days of the Revolution and so dragged nation and Empire to a future of woe and shame.'

One ought not to hold the politician to his words; he is not a calculating machine, which always gives the same answer. Still less to some one else's words. What matters is the atmosphere that is around him, that he makes around him. In 1920 in his paper the *Deutsche Stimmen* there appeared this poem:

Yours is our hate
Who broke the oath.
Ours is the hate
Of lies, of shame.
God has our prayers,

Who pays for sin,
That from our land
He drive you forth.
Yours is our hate
Who broke the oath,
Who greatly sinned
'Gainst God and King.

The period of unavoidable opposition because the People's Party was but a tiny group pressed forcibly towards the Right, is a romantic period. In the agitation which memory dedicated to the rich, the mighty past, the heart of the party leader beat in unison with those of his followers. To other parties let the future belong and the present ; there were one hundred thousand folk in Germany who held to the past out of loyalty, out of sentiment and because all was going ill with them in the new age. Should they be left without a struggle to the Nationalist Party ? Here was the store from which the People's Party could draw strength.

Stresemann had never become a Byzantine. He had all the pride of the middle class, even during the era of monarchy, and liked to show it. A portrait of Ernst August was once being auctioned in Weimar. The student of Goethe was there. He made his bid when with courtly dignity a chamberlain approached him. Would he withdraw, for the Grand Duke wanted the picture ? The deputy answered that he would go on bidding as long as his purse held out ; then he would stop. The picture was knocked down to him. There were many brave democrats, one feels, who would not have opposed the wish of his Royal Highness. The Order of the

White Falcon which beckoned alluringly in the background was coveted by a good many people. With princes who were Liberals he liked to be associated. He talked politics with the Grand Duke of Oldenburg, with the Duke of Schleswig-Holstein. The Emperor, whom in twenty-five years of public life Bassermann never saw, he did not know. He had, as we know, fiercely attacked him because Bülow was prevented from usefully serving his country. He spoke out bluntly: 'The wearer of the Crown lets himself be swayed by personal feeling to the detriment of the Empire.' He preferred Napoleon, who after the return from Elba called to his soldiers: 'Here I am, your old commander; fire on me if you wish.' 'Many a monarch would not have been abandoned by his troops and his people had he at the right moment behaved like that.' Yet on the Emperor's sixtieth birthday he sent a telegram to Amerongen. He went to Holland and visited the Crown Prince at Wieringen on the Zuider Zee. Propaganda needs were mingled with romantic sympathy.

At the same time he was doing hard practical work. He went up and down the country founding local party groups, choosing local secretaries, made his own the *Deutsche Stimmen*, then a much-read review which earlier had belonged to the party, and at the same time put the party on a firm basis and equally his own position in it. In the first Republican Reichstag which was elected on July 6, 1920, the numbers of the People's Party rose from twenty-two to sixty-five. Centrists and Democrats had shrunk; the Nationalists came back half as strong again. The People's Party had appreciably come nearer to being a centre party. When the Centrist leader Fehrenbach formed a new cabinet, the Saxon Heinze, the party's first president, was Vice-Chancellor and Minister of Justice in it.

Three great events give the years 1920 to 1923 their political character—the Kapp rising, Upper Silesia, and the Ruhr struggle.

When the East Prussian land official Kapp appointed himself Chancellor, the People's Party—this was before the elections—still stood well on the right of the parliamentary battle-line. Its propaganda still spent itself in praise of the old days, and from that it hoped for a great increase in seats and in influence, as it did actually obtain later on. It had passed the sharpest of judgements on the Republic, but in its dealings with the Republic had 'based itself on facts'. In the detailed report which later he made on 'the March revolt' he tells how, on the day of the outbreak, it was asserted that everywhere the soldiers were standing by Kapp's side. Calmly he replied, 'Just as on November 9, 1918, the country was confronted by a *de facto* power which it would have been well theoretically but was not practically possible to ignore,' and he called the 'putsch' 'criminal folly'. But he had no more approval for the general strike. For him all depended on the restoration of constitutionalism—by way of negotiation. The People's Party forbade its members to take office in Kapp's government, but Stresemann feared that, if the unions won, there would be a wave of Bolshevism and a workers' guard would be substituted for the Reichswehr. He saw that his task was to mediate. One remembers how the leaders of the bourgeois parties

—announced or not announced—had waited in the ante-room while Prince Max of Baden surrendered power to Ebert. The role of the People's Party in March 1920 was much the same. It was not yet in harmony with the new State, which had been founded, as it were, over its head. The time was not yet come when Stresemann was to be ready to defend the Republic with his life. He was still without power. What power he had had, he had lost. What power he had so far won under the Republic was very trifling, too trifling to let him have any legitimist feeling for the Republic.

. . . . .

By the terms of the Armistice, Germany had taken it upon herself to pay compensation for war damage done to civilians. The Allies added to that war pensions. No total liability, such as was fixed in the Peace of Frankfurt at the end of the Franco-German War of 1870–71, was fixed by the Versailles treaty. Twenty-seven international conferences sat one after another to try and discover a total, until finally the march into the Ruhr put an end to negotiation.

For many parties this was a time of mutual efforts to outdo each other in expression of nationalist feeling. None of them can do enough in the way of angry rejection of the Allied demands—when they are in opposition; each must bow to the inevitable and agree to dangerous concessions—if it is in power. There was certainly reason enough for anger. The sums demanded were fantastic in their magnitude, all the more fantastic because no one, neither in Paris nor in London, nor even Berlin, had any idea of what Germany really could pay. Germany was in a state of despair, production was only slowly getting under way again, the printing machines were working overtime to produce bank-notes, the mark was falling, and, in spite of inflation-dumping, the trade balance was badly against Germany. Wages and salaries steadily declined in purchasing power; the people were in dire distress.

The politicians could offer their constituents no stronger meat than exhibitions of anger over other peoples' willingness to pay and base servility. This was a time when legends were told abroad and found believers. Erzberger had sold the mercantile marine to the enemy. Rathenau was one of the three hundred 'sages of Zion' who were the real rulers of the world, and were resolved on Germany's destruction.

The phrases which prepared the way for the murder of these two men were coined now; the Nationalist terror was already abroad here and there; Captain Paasche and the Bavarian Social Democrat Gareis had already fallen victims to it. The murderers were not arrested. That later with the catch-word 'Stresemann — corpse-man'[1] the leader of the People's Party would be brought into the company of the threatened no one then could anticipate. Popular history still tells to-day, and will go on telling eternally, how the German leaders were divided into two camps. In one were servile pacifists who licked the boots of the French generals, and in the other upright patriots who opposed an obstinate 'No' to every demand of the Allies. Politics go in ways very different from those in which the picture-book illustrators like to make them run.

[1] *Verwesene* is an adjective applied to the putrescent corpse. The jingle which cannot be exactly reproduced in English amounted to incitement to murder (cf. p. 177.)—TRS.

From June 1920 the Fehrenbach cabinet remained in power for nearly a year, based on a Parliamentary minority of Centrists, Democrats, and People's Party. The People's Party was represented in the cabinet by Heinze, von Raumer, and Scholz, all belonging to its right wing. The Baden lawyer who, as Chancellor, directed policy was old and tired, a man of undoubted probity but exhausted and no longer possessed of creative energy, a wary parliamentary warrior but not accustomed to international negotiations. Simons, a jurist from the Foreign Office, a courteous gentleman, supple rather than courageous, a scholar rather than a politician, but a politician all the same, favourably regarded by public opinion as an 'expert', had won the confidence of the parties. He conducted foreign affairs independently. Proposals drawn up in Paris demanded two hundred and eighty-six thousand million marks. Simons offered fifty milliards in London. Whether or no an English suggestion prompted him has never been definitely cleared up. The Allies replied by an ultimatum demanding one hundred and thirty-two milliards. Simons said 'No'. When he returned to Berlin a crowd, wild with excitement and enthusiasm, met him at the Lehrter station. Although he was no strong character he had won a national reputation for firmness. But from the point of view of foreign politics he had done nothing except run on the rocks. In his extremity he turned to the Pope, to President Harding, for intervention, mediation. In vain. The cabinet resigned.

Stresemann took its fall very calmly, with a calmness which is impressive, for three of his own Party friends belonged to it, as calmly indeed as

Simons's reception in Berlin had been the reverse of calm. He wrote: 'The Fehrenbach-Simons cabinet fell on the American note. It had begun on its own responsibility a great foreign political negotiation, and after the failure of its method confidence in it was so rudely shaken that it had no longer authority to carry on the government. Without touching too closely on individuals who, besides, would be attacked as leaders of the government, it may be said of the cabinet in its final period: It had no luck.'

One remembers that once before he had said that about a government. Then it was of Bethmann-Hollweg's. One must not push parallels too far. His opposition to Simons is nothing like his opposition to Bethmann. But it was strong enough. Between Simons the patrician, the conservative in inclination and feeling, and the son of the 'Budiker', the parvenu, there could be no sympathy. Stresemann felt that. But above all he knew from his own experience how cheaply the fruit of the tree of public popularity may be plucked if one plays the stout hero, the man who never surrenders, instead of seeking to carry out a practical policy. And so he asked in doubt whether the 'connexions' which should have saved Germany from ultimatum, had been 'carefully and cleverly enough secured'.

The resignation of the Government created a situation that was clearly an opportunity for a politician who had confidence in his own courage and ability to take up again the reparations discussions, to secure the final liquidation of the war and raise Germany from the depths.

On May 4th the Fehrenbach cabinet had resigned.

A SILVER WEDDING GROUP

A PHOTOGRAPH TAKEN AT WIESBADEN IN OCTOBER 1928

Left to right: Secretary of Legation Baron von Maltzan, Dr. Wolfgang Stresemann (eldest son), Frau Stresemann, Herr Stresemann, Secretary of Legation Dr. Feine, Herr Joachim Stresemann (younger son)

On May 5th the Entente ultimatum arrived in Berlin with a time-limit of six days. For six days Germany had a respite. On May 11th it must either be accepted or 'sanctions' would be applied, new sanctions, crueller, harder to be borne than before. Several Rhineland towns, including Düsseldorff and Duisburg, had already been occupied in March. Now France stood armed and ready to march into the Ruhr.

Germany was once again threatened, worse threatened than ever before in the cruel years that had succeeded the conclusion of peace. While the hardest question of all demanded an answer, Germany was without a government. A cabinet of some kind must assume office. The President of the Republic, Ebert, went looking for a Chancellor.

Still another problem stood in the background. In March the plebiscite had taken place in Upper Silesia. It was to provide a basis for the decision whether that valuable territory should in future belong to Germany or to Poland. How would the balance fall? The vote of the Upper Silesian population had not been so clear that in the existing relations of the powers different interpretations could not be put upon it. Above all, the fate of the industrial triangle Kattowitz-Gleiwitz-Königshütte was at stake. It was a necessary condition of Germany's existence that she possess it.

While Ebert was looking for a man to take upon himself the terrible burden of responsibility, while the Parliamentary Parties were arguing, valuable time was being lost. Opinions on acceptance or rejection did not follow rigid left and right lines as the propagandists were afterwards to declare. The situation would have been considerably simpler if it had been so. But in national crises the dividing line runs not between, but through, the parties. The Democrats were divided and so were the People's Party. Even for the Social Democrats unity was obtained only after a struggle. Even among the Nationalists there were deputies who thought that yielding to the ultimatum was inevitable. First of all the Centrists gained unity. Their representatives in the Inter-Party Commission handed in a declaration that the party would vote for acceptance. That was on May 8th.

On May 9th Stresemann appeared at the British Embassy. The Ambassador, Lord d'Abernon, was still in London. His deputy, Lord Kilmarnock, received the party leader. He spoke, as Lord Kilmarnock's telegram to London says, 'with great earnestness and moderation and in a thoroughly business-like spirit'. He asked four questions and desired an immediate answer. Two were concerned with the conditions for German deliveries and the exports duties—to-day these have lost whatever significance they had and are indeed scarcely comprehensible. The third was whether, if the ultimatum was accepted, Düsseldorf and Duisburg, the 'sanction towns', which had been occupied after the London conference, would be evacuated. The fourth was the most important. How was the plebiscite in Upper Silesia to be considered? Would Germany receive the industrial area?

It seems that Stresemann took the same step at the Italian Embassy. On the results of his negotiations with the British the memoirs of Lord d'Abernon give precise information. The Ambassador returned on the same day as Stresemann had visited his deputy. He sent a second dispatch on the heels of Kilmarnock's which emphasized the importance of the event. The answer came on May 10th. It was favourable as far as the first three points were concerned, dubious, but not actually hostile, on the fourth.

On the 11th[1] in the early part of the day on which the ultimatum expired, d'Abernon received Stresemann and communicated the result to him. 'Never did the communication of a diplomatic document cause greater emotion,' notes d'Abernon in his diary. The day before, the Wirth cabinet had taken office. It was composed of Social Democrats, Democrats, and Centrists. This was the 'Weimar coalition', the coalition of July 1917. Wirth called his cabinet 'the cabinet of fulfilment'. The People's Party was not represented in it. The offer to include Dr. Heinze as Minister of Justice was roundly and without discussion refused by the Parliamentary Party. What would have a minor post under the leadership of the republican Catholic Wirth have signified? For the party nothing. For Stresemann less than nothing. But if the British answer had come but two days earlier everything would have been different. The Upper Silesian question was not decided approximately so much in Germany's favour as the statement of Curzon had let men hope, as Stresemann had taken as certain, after the Ambassador had read to him the telegram from London. But at the moment Stresemann had some title to believe that the industrial district would remain in Germany, and did believe so. He believed that Britain had decided on this point and that he himself

[1] D'Abernon in the *Diary* says the 12th.—TRS.

was the man who had produced the decision. The exchange of telegrams had been as rapid as could have been conceived. Why had he not put his questions three, two days earlier? Then he could have gone before the Parliamentary Party with the costly treasure of this promise: the recalcitrant would have voted for the acceptance of the ultimatum; the hesitant would have followed his lead, and he himself would have taken over the task of cabinet-making.

Stresemann, let us remember, had been aghast when Erzberger reported on the terrible state of things at the front in March 1917, when the Reichstag came to grips with the problem of driving the Army Command from power. He had seemed on the verge of a seizure when Major von dem Bussche announced defeat, when he finally realized what an historic opportunity had been definitely lost. Through a mountain of difficulties against open hostility and concealed enmities, he had set to work to raise up a party that had been brought low, in order to get within nearer reach of power. When at last he reached out his hand to grasp it, it was too late. 'It appeared to me,' wrote d'Abernon, 'that what was going through Stresemann's mind was the reflection that, had the answer—so unexpectedly favourable in its tenor—been received forty-eight hours sooner, there would not have been a Wirth cabinet, but a Stresemann cabinet.'

The favourable answer of the British Foreign Minister had been unexpected. If things turned out in Upper Silesia as the answer allowed men to hope, it would be the Chancellor of the new cabinet who would be able to give a tremendous national satisfaction to Germany. The milliards which were demanded in the London ultimatum were not taken seriously by any one who was in close touch with politics and had had experience of that endless series of conferences. D'Abernon did not take them seriously, nor did Stresemann, nor did the two hundred and twenty deputies who on the evening of that very 11th May voted for acceptance of the ultimatum, nor yet the one hundred and seventy-two deputies who voted against it. All thought that they had reason to believe that the total would again, and yet again, be revised.

But Upper Silesia, the industrial jewel in Germany's crown: Stresemann thought that he held that too in the hollow of his hand when he heard Curzon's message. And at that very hour it was torn from him. The liberator of the national territory—that is what he believed he could have been then, that was what he became later after so many fresh struggles and trials. Wirth, the Christian Socialist, had allied himself with the other Socialists, had taken the clever step of voluntarily accepting the responsibility which seemed so heavy. The day before he had become Chancellor; to-day he would induce the Reichstag to action which seemed dangerous and should now be a bringer of good fortune. The People's Party stood aside. At its head Stresemann could have done the same with a light heart, could have been the leader who conducted Germany to a better future. The words in d'Abernon's diary, though extraordinary, are no exaggeration: 'Never did the communication of a diplomatic document cause greater emotion.'

CHAPTER VI

DAMASCUS

STRESEMANN had wanted to take over the Government. He found it difficult to stand aside any longer. D'Abernon notes: 'My impression is that the People's Party have an ardent desire to join the Government.' Stresemann said at the time: 'The bread of government responsibility is much more bitter to eat than the sweet manna of opposition.' But however justified the saying may be, it had nothing to do with the present situation. After the great victory at the Reichstag elections of 1920, the still greater one at the Prussian polls in 1921, after the heavy losses of the Independent Socialists and the Democrats, the People's Party was no longer a party of the Right. According to Stresemann's view it should not be. The facts which were stronger than he had temporarily made it so. As he defined its status it was 'a Right party of the centre'. The adjective was a concession to the electors and to the strength of the party in Parliament and in the country. He would have wished that it could be just a centre party. 'People's commonwealth', 'the unity of the national front' were his oft-repeated slogans; he turned the pressure put upon the State into an argument for the necessity of unity, of concentration. But that was a pretext, a view that arose from sentiment and did not inspire it. It was not an idea forced upon him. He dreamed of, he loved the 'people's commonwealth' and his party as the centre party in it.

At this time oppositions were effaced which earlier would have meant a split. Its monarchist leanings, wrote Stresemann, ought not to prevent the Social Democrats from forming a coalition with the People's Party. They have no actual significance; they are not 'fundamentally different conceptions'. Herr Scheidemann, a Republican, could enter an Imperial cabinet. The distinction was so clear, so obvious, that it could not be missed. The rejection of the ultimatum by the party—did that really signify anything? The majority of the Democrats had also decided against it. He sharply criticized 'the silly folk' who declared that his attitude in the war made him an unsuitable person for international negotiations; the British and the French preferred to negotiate with nationalists rather than with pacifists. And then the economic party, the party of industry, ought to be a negotiating party; its signature meant more to the Entente than that of any other. It is interesting to note that the same argument appears in the conversation with the British Ambassador. But it was not d'Abernon who used it; it was Stresemann. The Ambassador indeed was rather doubtful about it. The monarchism of the People's Party disturbed him; he preferred to see Wirth Chancellor rather than any other.

What attracted Stresemann thus to power, to a responsibility which was so difficult to carry? Ambition? The word has a tang about it. It is used to expose vanity, to convey criticism. But the feeling that one has a vocation is really the same thing. The legend of the Emperor Henry whom the message from the birds overtook, is it not a pious fiction ? Did not the Emperor intend all the time that the longed-for message should come to him.

There is only one apology for ambition, and when it is made no other need be offered. He who is ambitious must do the work better, must seem more a chosen vessel than the others.

Stresemann's opposition, his criticism, again became sharper. It was directed partly against Wirth, the new Chancellor. His temperament, his lack of restraint, his radicalism, these, said Stresemann warningly, were dangerous symptoms. He warned the Centrists. Wirth's policy was directed against his own party. And most dangerous of all, there, in the background, was Erzberger. The Chancellor was nothing—his pupil, his junior. Erzberger had had to clear himself of a charge of corruption by his action against Helfferich, by an unpleasant action. Some mud inevitably stuck.

He had had to withdraw from public life so long as the suspicion of perjury hung over him. After the verdict he returned to address mass meetings which loudly cheered him ; he returned to political life. A good many of the Centrists did not like the idea. Stresemann raised a warning finger : Protect yourselves. By his attacks on Wirth he sought to keep Erzberger off the political stage ; by warning the nation against Erzberger, he sought to undermine Wirth's position. The sanctions, wrote Stresemann on July 17, 1921, have not yet been revoked. Things in Upper Silesia are as confused as ever. Even if the French withdraw their representative at Oppeln, General le Rond, and replace him by a civilian, nothing will thereby be altered. 'The revenge-seeking lieutenant of the vain and blustering Briand'—this is surely not from his pen, for that is not his tone even when he is roused—was the name already given to the French commissioner in Stresemann's review. And here too—though Stresemann anticipates—Wirth had no success.

Erzberger fell. While on a walk at Griesbach in the Black Forest, where he had gone for a brief holiday before he moved to the attack, Nationalists shot him dead. The shadow which the threatening presence of murderers ready to kill was already casting over Germany grew darker, more menacing. The deed was not the result of a simple explosion of national feeling; it was part of a conspiracy of murder. The terror raised its bloodstained hand. An obituary article by Stresemann brought up all the reproaches which he could bring against the dead man, his old opponent.

Once again, as in the year after the revolution, he became bitter. After a visit to Weimar he remembered the quotation from Goethe which Ebert had used at the opening of the National Assembly, and said in mockery: 'The worship of the great prophet of the spirit should be opposed to spiritual militarism.' And alluding to the burglaries and robberies which had been occurring at Weimar and which were rousing feeling all over Germany because of the associations of the place, he said: 'The old Germany protected the treasures of Weimar. The new Government of the spirit seems unable to prevent the Tierfurt from being burgled and thieves from entering and plundering the Roman House and the Mausoleum.' There could hardly be a more

biased or a more unjust accusation. Elsewhere there are pretty passages in this 'Weimar diary', full of love and admiration for the revered poet. All seems peaceful, and then suddenly the anger breaks forth. No more is said of people's commonwealths, of the sharing of responsibility, of only 'fundamental' differences of opinion. The other party is simply wrong, guilty.

Then when an appeal comes from the Nationalists to join them in an attack he returns suddenly to sober sense. No, the centre must rule. How his combativeness, his rudeness impressed men is seen in the *Frankfurter Zeitung's* remark that it could not understand how the People's Party put up with Stresemann as its leader. About the same time d'Abernon noted: 'I gather that Stresemann does not propose to take office. . . . The reasons given are that his wild, untamable nature is unsuited to the trammels of official life. . . . The real reason is that he would not take anything less than the Chancellorship. Unquestionably a big man and he knows it.'

It was a period not indeed of inactivity but of vain excitement, a wearing time. Stresemann's temperament urged him forward, his gaze was turned to distant horizons; goals which were very far away he saw close at hand. He had been cast down and at once had bent all his efforts to recover lost ground. That had been quickly, unexpectedly quickly, accomplished. Now he felt neglected again. He had thought of conquering power simultaneously with winning a great national victory; the hope was disappointed. There came years in which things went ill with State and people. Many a time it seemed as if they would end in the abyss. Others were in power in whose spirit and character he did not have unshakable confidence. He had trusted once, he had been loyal and true—and he had suffered disillusionment. Since then he was mistrustful. He would not have been the leader he was had he not believed that he could render his people better service than any one else.

In 1921 Joseph Wirth had taken over the Government. A head teacher from Freiburg in the Breisgau, fair, youthful, beaming all over, capable of inspiration, of inspiring, very like Hellriegel in Gerhart Hauptmann's winter's tale, fresh and open in countenance: so he seemed to many. But Stresemann thought that his policy was not as ingenuous as the casual observer might think; he found something crafty about such complete and childlike innocence.

His political career had often been hard. He had suffered many a reverse. In the future there were to be bitter hours in which all he had secured seemed vain and useless. But the worst of all was these years of waiting, of looking on, of semi-activity. The party leader who now will content himself only with the highest office, the Chancellorship, 'a big man and he knows it', began the draft of an autobiographical novel. He never finished it. Opposition—that was the worst of it—could only be half opposition. Stresemann had to remember that if the ultimatum had been rejected by a section of his party, it had been accepted by important members of the Parliamentary Party. Fundamentally he could not oppose acceptance. He knew, and had impressed it upon his party comrades, that Germany must fulfil her obligations as far as her strength permitted. As a result of his initiative the Great Coalition had become a fact in the Prussian Parliament. There Socialists and People's Party ruled together. That tied the hands of the party in the national parliament, for here too a similar solution might any day be found. It is impossible to burn up in the evening what one has worshipped in the morning. Stresemann guarded himself well. 'We must not reproach British parliamentarians for the many contradictions that are found between their words and their actions, if such contradictions appear to them necessary in order to attain the goal they have set for themselves.'

But it was not the case here that a contradiction made for tactical reasons could be denounced next day without paying the penalty for it. The lack of restraint with which, later, the Nationalist opposition was to resist Stresemann as Minister did not then lie within the realm of likely possibility. The responsibility for not being in the Government lay on his own shoulders. To-morrow he might well be, and then he would have to carry out what yesterday he had opposed. He warned his party friends. It was unwise to obey any impulse that might prevent a policy of fight. He was impetuous, hot-blooded, 'wild', as people told d'Abernon. But now he must only gnash his teeth, not bite with them.

He had had to let the desire go for a 'people's commonwealth', for 'a national front'. He was now the man of the coalition which should embrace Left and Centre, Socialists, Democrats, Centrists, and People's Party. If it came to pass, he was its leader, and not either Heinze or Scholz, who were in the right wing of the party. A great speech was devoted to defending the Government to which he did not belong, to extolling the great coalition which others did not wish to make. That was on December 1, 1921, at the party conference in Stuttgart. He had built up the party out of the opponents of the Republic, malcontents, and panegyrists of the ancient times. He had now to tell them that the time had come for the party to assume the leadership of the Republic. A brilliant speech, magnificent in construction. From 'the violation of right of Versailles' to 'Deutschland über alles', every national note was struck which could serve the orator in his campaign for unity, and all were struck to carry his audience with him. The Party leader went far back. What he had said in 1906 to the middle-class Liberals at the Goslar conference before he had become the youngest member of the Reichstag, that they lacked the will to power, he brought back out of the past and placed in the clear light of the present. The Socialists had fought for their ideas; the Conservatives had ruthlessly asserted themselves. But the Liberals had only and always shown weakness, and so misfortune had overtaken Germany. Shall it be so again because the party wastes its strength mourning what has been lost? Now he speaks no longer of the dreams of the Sabbath hours, which are devoted to the past. That was all right when the party was small and was driven to the Right by the powerful masses of the Left. To-day it was a big party and stood in a central position. 'Are we not again in the position of simply following events when we ought to be seizing opportunity by the forelock? Shall we again watch others hold power in the State because we cannot rise to the deliberate placing of our seal on circumstances?' The applause was loud. Whatever their private resentments, that the delegates did understand. And as he coveted power for the party he demanded the leadership for himself. 'If you place any one at the head of a party, then you ought not to seek to restrict him in any way at decisive moments, for you must also suffer that man, if he is a personality, to use his personality in order to bring his ideas to fruition.' Again a roar of applause greeted him. It was full powers that the conference gave him to lead the party from its opposition to fulfilment into the Government and to place himself at its head. But two years passed before Stresemann could make use of these full powers: two years' perseverance, two years' patience, two years' waiting in a life whose allotted span was too short to allow it to waste years. Two years' support of what others did and did not do well; two years of simple onlooking as Germany's path led downward; two years to be fooled by fate.

The decision on the partition of Upper Silesia fell to the League of Nations Council. The dollar in Berlin rose from 150 marks to 185. The first Wirth cabinet resigned. The national feeling was so convinced that the policy of fulfilment was not possible of execution without the possession of the industrial part of Upper Silesia that the Democrats had left the coalition.

Wirth formed a new ministry of Social Democrats and Centrists. The political centre of gravity instead of going Right had gone farther to the Left.

A great taxation scheme called 'the tax compromise', which meant heavy sacrifices from owners of property, was accepted by the People's Party. Again, in January 1922, the Great Coalition appeared to be near realization. The Chancellor promised the People's Party that negotiations would begin in a day or two. But the next thing that happened was the appointment of Rathenau as Foreign Minister. 'At a time,' wrote Stresemann, 'when it had been expressly demanded by the Parliamentary Party that an appointment to this post should not be made except in complete agreement with it.' He felt himself over-reached. He complained bitterly: 'The Moor has done his work; the Moor can go.'

The Genoa conference meant a pause in the development of the political situation at home. The dollar rose to 1,300 marks. The conclusion of the treaty of Rapallo between Germany and Russia was satisfaction to German self-esteem, but it made no difference to the reparations position.

On June 24, 1922, Rathenau was shot dead by members of a Fascist secret society. The dollar rose to 350 marks, on July 1st to 400, on July 7th to 500. The law for the protection of the Republic announced as a means of repression of the Nationalist terror was also accepted by the People's Party. Stresemann wanted it to be called the law for the protection of the Constitution, a formal phrase which revealed the fact that he was making a fighting retreat to the line of the Republic.

But the Majority Socialists united now with the Independent Socialists and the centre of gravity moved again to the Left. The Chancellor in the Reichstag cried angrily: 'The enemy is on the

Right.' The Great Coalition seemed farther away than ever.

The negotiations on reparations after Rathenau's death went backward rather than forward. The dollar rose to 4,000 marks, when the dispute over the presidency arose. Ebert was ruthlessly attacked by the Nationalists because he had clung to office although established in it only for the period of the National Assembly. They wished to make Hindenburg president. Stresemann wanted Bülow to become head of the State. Shortly before he had greeted him ' in the hope that an opportunity would be given him to serve his people and his fatherland in that spirit of the Fatherland which had been the inspiration of his whole life and character '. He was always inclined to worship personality, and here he was true to it. But he saw that between Left and Right Bülow's candidature was hopeless. The law which made Ebert's continuance in office constitutional owed its passing to Stresemann.

Once again he had rendered a service to that Government coalition which began only to the left of his own party. It was the party comrades of the President who shrank from prolonging his term of office. They feared that in these difficult times too much of their party's prestige would be lost. Stresemann said to Lord d'Abernon : ' I am almost certain that I can get the Socialist parties in to agree. Should it go through, I believe the People's Party will join the Government, or rather I should have believed it, had it not been so near coming through on four previous occasions. Whenever we get to that stage something happens.' Contrary as it was to his nature, he indulged in forebodings : ' Whenever we get to this stage, something happens. The first time there was the Kapp putsch, the next time Erzberger was murdered, the third time poor Rathenau fell. He was still suspicious: 'I am not sure how far Wirth really wants us. We party leaders do not think him quite straight.'[1]

The British observer, with the cold unsentimental regard of a Roman, saw that his German visitor was fundamentally altering his tone. He remarked that he was 'more urbane', and noted: 'His voice is less resonant and metallic and he no longer commences as if he were addressing a public meeting.'

That was in the second half of October. Only a week later, when the dollar rose to 7,000 marks, Wirth resigned again. The attempt to solve the reparations problem had failed; the finances of the Republic had collapsed owing to the depreciation of the mark.

In November 1922 the President of the Republic called to the Chancellorship the general manager of the Hamburg-America Line, Cuno.

Ebert's choice of men did not always escape criticism. This time, however, the German preference for the expert made it admired. Cuno, although not so long ago a privy councillor in a Government department, had the reputation of being a great economic authority and of being an important link with the United States. To this man of the world was added as Foreign Minister a professional diplomatist, Rosenberg. Their ministry lasted till August 1923.

Now began the last heroic period in the recent history of Germany. The hero is not the new

[1] Cf. d'Abernon's *Diary*, ii, p. 115.

Chancellor, the elegant general manager from Hamburg, still less the arid official who occupied the Foreign Office; the hero is the working-class of the Ruhr, the great mass of the German workers and officials, the German middle class. The German people, who for half a century had been accustomed to play an active part in battle, turned in despair to passive heroism.

Stresemann's reception of the Cuno-Rosenberg cabinet was icy in its coldness. He compared it to the government of Michaelis. When the head of the Food Department had become the occupant of the Chancellery, whose political incapacity was just as proverbial as the 'hundred days' of this Bible student-chancellor, there could not be 'days of national uplifting'. He wrote: 'There are situations in which anything new seems to lighten the burden because there is no longer any confidence in the success of the old. In that situation the ex-general manager of the Hamburg-America Line took over the Government.' One could hardly say more plainly how little belief one had in the success of the new men.

If that meant, as was generally understood, mistrust in Cuno and Rosenberg, the situation none the less made it imperative that the leader of the People's Party should show parliamentary confidence in them. That two of his party colleagues, Heinze and Becker, were in the cabinet was significant. Something else also held his hand. He clearly explained what: 'In the next weeks within a short time it will be necessary as far as foreign politics are concerned to stand as far as is possible united and unanimous.' The choice of Cuno meant that an attempt was to be made to conduct policy by other methods ; that meant war, if war of a special and extraordinary kind. The French made good the threat that they had always made, and marched into the Ruhr, and there the passive resistance began. It was war, and Stresemann intended to support the leaders with all his strength, just as he had done in the Great War. Only this time he was on his guard. He kept his eyes open and did not give his confidence blindly. His tendency to romance a second time rose high, but his practical hold on men and things did not relax for a second.

The diplomatic notes of the Cuno government failed to conceal what was coming. France complained in the Reparations Commission that Germany was defaulting in her deliveries of coal and timber. The default was barely a two per cent one, but it sufficed. The Commission declared that 'failure to fulfil' was the same as 'deliberate default'. That was enough to justify 'sanctions'. France announced that a commission of engineers would be sent into the Ruhr to survey the activities of the Coal Combine. Those engineers needed military protection. Military protection for a few engineers meant the advance of a quarter of a million troops, with guns, aircraft, and tanks. It meant the severance of all trade communication with the occupied territory, the seizure of German public moneys, the expulsion of German officials, firing on German workmen, and fantastic sentences on German industrialists.

The Government allowed the Ruhr to stop work. That meant that the fifty millions in unoccupied Germany would have to feed the ten millions in the occupied territory. When on January 10th the first French division marched in the dollar was worth 10,000 marks. On January 31st it was worth 50,000. The Reichsbank threw its gold into the battle and drove the dollar down to 20,000 and kept it there until April. Then the unequal struggle ended in defeat. The dollar rose catastrophically in May to 50,000 marks, in June to 100,000, in July to 300,000, in August to 4,000,000.

A vision indeed of hell. The people knew starvation as in the last years of the war; the profiteers exulted; the combines of great industrialists grew to giant size. What the middle class had saved, gained, inherited, hoarded, the strongest buttress of the State's existence, melted away, disappeared into nothingness, vanished from the world as a dream that is dreamt. In the British House of Commons the pacifist Morel called the passive resistance 'the greatest demonstration of moral force against military aggression that history can show'.

In March of the Ruhr year 1923, Rosenberg, the Foreign Minister, announced to the British Ambassador that, if the Cuno government did not succeed in obtaining the evacuation of the Ruhr, then civil war would assuredly break out in a few months' time. Any coalition with the Social Democrats would end in a rising. Any premature attempt to negotiate with the French could only lead to trouble either from the Left or from the Right. The fall of the Government would be the prelude to revolution.

In April, Stresemann said to d'Abernon that abandonment of the passive resistance was only possible after the French troops had left the Ruhr. The Social Democrat deputy, Breitscheid, and Georg Bernhard, the editor-in-chief of the *Vossische Zeitung*, who were present at the conversation and were ' the most thorough supporters of a policy of compromise ', did not contradict him.

In May the Government made a new reparations offer to the Allies. Rosenberg declared that only the Cuno government could have gone so far. If Wirth had made it, he would have gone in danger of his life. If Breitscheid had made it, Bavaria would have left the Republic. Only he and Cuno stood between Germany and ruin. D'Abernon, the unsentimental observer, remarked that every minister willingly believes that, if he gives up the government, the result will be catastrophe. But all the same he agreed with Rosenberg's forecast. On August 7th the Minister said : ' We have no longer a choice between capitulation and chaos. There is no such alternative. Capitulation is chaos.'

For Stresemann, with his strongly Nationalist feelings, his own vehemence of nature, his brilliant urge to activity, no time could have been more captivating than this time of the passive resistance. But he felt the fascination of it only at moments. Years had passed since he had delivered those clarion war speeches of his. With the historic situation he too had been transformed. He had for long, too long, reckoned that to-morrow he could surely be able to say from the ministerial bench what to-day he was saying from a deputy's seat, that to-morrow he would receive in the Chancellery the Ambassador who had read yesterday the words of an independent writer. It was war again. But this war of suffering, of passiveness, a war fought only with weapons of the spirit, was just what would rouse the patriot, who had learned that in war-time one must never forget the coming peace. D'Abernon, who saw Stresemann for the first time in 1921, has said that he had become a very different man. How much greater must the change in him have appeared to those who had known him in the world war.

In subdued tones he greeted 1923. The turn of the year he called a turning-point of destiny. He knew well enough what was going to happen. Only 'the ideas of German philistinism' could believe that the word 'struggle' meant simply the struggle of one party against another—struggle for seats in Parliament, for the supremacy of one party. Nay, these party struggles are only what their enemies call *querelles allemande*. Now, it was Germany's whole political future that was at stake, and internal political differences seemed very trifling things; viewed objectively they simply did not exist. That would have the sound of a war speech had it not been delivered with far greater earnestness, almost with grief. The word 'Ireland' is uttered to recall an example of the power of the idea. But then 'sacrifices, sacrifices'. The appeal was made to men of property.

The Cuno government knew no better how to deal with them than Helfferich had done when he was Finance Minister in the days of the world war. 'Sacrifices must be made, for we have lost the war.'

Once his temperament broke through the barriers, but that was only an episode. 'How long has the German nation longed for opposition somewhere to be made to that procedure, unexampled and unexcelled in insolence and impudence, to bear which in patience is so often amongst us held to be statesmanship?'

Only once. In these months popularity was the cheapest of all commodities; with the slightest of efforts a demagogue could have done excellent trade. Every day brought material for fiery speeches. No one could have used it so easily as Stresemann; no one had heart so filled and tongue so ablaze with the fire of nationalism as he. But through these months of horror he kept the beating of the drum subdued. Every sentence which he wrote and spoke was a renunciation of a cheap triumph. He argued with Poincaré about frontiers and military invasions. He knew—and was right—that economically the French action had failed. But he never spoke of a German victory. 'If to-day the desire is to rouse the German nation, that is very easy,' he said. But he preferred to meet the attacks of the Nationalist Party rather than do the easy thing. The nervous strength required for passive resistance means a far greater call on effort than does active resistance. He felt that himself, his own nerves were racked with those of the poor devils who were bearing the real burden of the struggle. So he refused to break into the rolling thunder and flashing lightning of Nationalist oratory. 'What will happen is veiled in deep darkness.'

He advised, he warned. There was nothing to be gained with the proud slogan, 'No negotiations.' German propaganda was needed in other countries. The notes of Herr Rosenberg were only propaganda for the Germans. He felt in anticipation the fate that threatened him, for he had come through suffering to knowledge, the fate that had already overtaken others when he said: 'A truth never prevails unless those who utter it bear persecution like the heretics.' For his own followers he is still the national leader, 'the German man', in spite of Westarp and more than he. But doubt creeps over him whether he will remain so.

To a French journalist who called on him he said: 'We must understand each other you and we. Otherwise we are both lost, and Europe with us.' 'And Stinnes?' said the doubting Frenchman. 'Ah, Stinnes,' answered Stresemann, 'a business man who is out for profits.' The merchant from Mülheim was then believed to be the real Emperor of Germany and Stresemann was thought to be of his retinue. But Stinnes' influence had long ceased to be so powerful, at least after 1920, when the great speculator was offered the Ministry of Transport and refused it. 'It was a great disillusionment for the party when the leader in the economic world decided for the latter in the conflict between politics and economics.' That was what Stresemann had written at the time.

He now got angry at the idle gossip about dictatorship which was heard so constantly at the café tables, although he was himself one of their gods. He quoted Goethe: 'Even in dangers I will not become foolishly impetuous.' His own thought is similar when in his soreness he said: 'There is left only a very narrow path along which we can go to make possible a resumption of negotiations.'

He had stood ready so long. Toilsomely and painfully had he striven to prepare the Great Coalition which would bring him to power. Now when passive resistance threatened to break down, when the tanks were parked all over the Ruhr, when the sunny Cuno and the dark Rosenberg seemed to be sinking into gentle slumber, now it seemed to him that the long-awaited was at hand. There is nothing of the pose of the man about to become a minister about him when he wrote: 'Only a fool can believe that any inner longing can lead a man to covet a ministerial seat.'

'The conditions are such that there can hardly be any one whose interests would be served by coveting the office of the Chancellor or the post of a minister.' When a weekly paper of the Left, the *Welt am Montag*, hailed him as the coming man, he angrily rejected the unsolicited testimonial. To the Social Democratic leader Hermann Müller, who at last was ready for the Great Coalition, he said sceptically that unity must be attained on all questions of policy before a new cabinet was formed.

On August 11th Stresemann was asked to form a new cabinet; on the 12th it was ready. He himself took over the Foreign Office and stayed there till his death. There is no doubt that he is where he has striven to be ever since a parliamentary regime had been established in Germany, perhaps long before that. But never had a goal, when reached, so fallen in value.

Stresemann's beginnings had been easy. When he came out of the narrow confines to which he was born without influence or connexions there had been general surrender to his ability and his strength of character. From the University to the industrial organization, from a secretaryship to the Reichstag, from mild rebellion to the confidence of the leader of the party, from being the Benjamin of Parliament to being one of its most prominent members; work, negotiation, political campaigns, chairmanships, flaming platform speeches, his inborn gifts made nothing seem difficult. Then came the period of reverses. The terrible shocks of the years 1917 and 1918, the painful rejection of him when the great Democratic Party was founded.

But once again he rose rapidly after he had gathered himself again together. But a second rise after a fall takes greater effort, demands more of heart and nerve than the first easy rise.

Then came the worst of all, the years of waiting, of standing in readiness, of non-admission. Once on a time it had been a matter of joyously going with the rest and advancing stormily. Now between affirmation and denial, between supporting and opposing the Government, there is only weary beating about. That had exhausted still more his youthful courage and forward striving. At last power came to him but no one else wanted it. There was no opposition to fight, no last battle to win was needed.

His ambition had been to ride magnificently into the castle of his dreams. And what had happened? Hesitatingly he strode over ruins to rule the land that Bismarck had ruled. Was that dream really dreamed in the tiny room behind the beer-parlour? Did it seem too bold, too ambitious, too fantastic? Did inspiration to complete the work of the Paulskirche, live under the black, red, and gold flag? If an oracle had prophesied to the child or to the youth what would really happen, perhaps he would have remained in the beer-shop or in the modest offices of the chocolate manufacturers.

A castle had raised its towers before his dream, blazing with light, marbled, stoutly built, dwelt in by happy folk guarded by shining armour. Imagination had gazed at it from far distances with eyes hot with longing. Now when he had crossed the threshold—had a *fata Morgana* deluded him ? Through dreary windows rustled bats ; the foot sank deep in slime ; rats and mice crawled about ; behind the gaping walls lurked skulking robbers with drawn swords and rifles cocked. Through the darkness came the moaning and the whimpering of a starving folk covered with ulcers and sores. The smell of a corpse filled the air.

When Stresemann's cabinet was appointed public opinion set it a double task—first to restore the currency, second to maintain the passive resistance. Nothing short of squaring the circle was asked of him. So long as the passive resistance ate like a cancer into the national finances, so long as unlimited, illimitable, payments flowed into the Ruhr as subsidies to a population undermined by idleness, so long as it was poured into this Danaids' cask, so long was every attempt to check the printing of bank-notes doomed in advance to failure. Two days before the change of government Stresemann had declared in the Reichstag that the resistance could not, would not, ought not to, be given up. In Stuttgart, in a great speech which was listened to by a world public, he now announced : 'Our next task—or rather the next but one—is to create a stable currency for Germany.' The next but one—the Chancellor meant that the sequence of events would have to be different from what the public thought, that his task was more difficult than he had said.

The passive resistance had been a symbol of the

national strength ; it had become an idol. Although in the Ruhr itself almost every belief that it could last had vanished, in the rest of Germany men stood firmly by it. After the defeat of the world war, after four years of simple endurance, it seemed an act of heroism at which the national spirit could be kindled afresh. When a Rhinelander, a member of the People's Party, had said, 'The Bavarians will fight on to the last Rhinelander', the bitter jest did not apply only to Bavarians. If it became known that the resistance had been nothing more than a demonstration on a large scale, then the disillusion would be bitter, perhaps intolerable. For months the Press had dinned it into the ears of the people : the French cannot get our railways going, they cannot make our factories work, they will freeze because they cannot get coal from our mines. But what would happen if the railways did run again, if the machinery started again, if coal came up again from the pit, and the French machine-guns, cannon, and tanks were still unwithdrawn, standing just where they had always stood ? What could a politician expect who took the responsibility for that upon himself ?

On the day when Stresemann took over the government things had come to such a pass that civil peace was seriously threatened. The printers had struck and the bank-note presses ceased to produce ; there was no more money to be had. If the strike had not been quickly ended civil war would have been inevitable.

In Berlin the Communist Committee of Fifteen gave the signal for a general strike.

Hunger riots in the provinces were a common

occurrence. In Gelsenkirchen, Hanover, Neurode in Silesia, Stettin, and Halle shops were plundered and police fired on the rioters. Dead and wounded lay on the streets. That was the news on the day, the 12th of August, on which Stresemann became Chancellor. On the succeeding days the messages were the same, only the names of the towns were different.

In Bavaria the Nationalist 'fighting associations' armed themselves. In Saxony proletarian 'hundreds' were formed.

On the last day of office of the Cuno cabinet the dollar in Berlin rose to 5,000,000 marks. After the change of government it fell to 3,000,000, and was held at that level for a couple of days. At end of August it was worth 10,000,000 marks, and in September rose to twenty, thirty, fifty, ninety millions. In the middle of the month it was worth 180,000,000 marks.

On August 11th, when Cuno resigned, President Ebert, speaking at a public demonstration, said: 'Never yet has a victor intoxicated with victory maintained his position; world history teaches us that.' That no victor could maintain his position; that was spoken for the Ruhr war.

Stresemann was received as Chancellor with mistrust by the Right. The *Kreuzzeitung* wrote of the 'ambitious politician whose dream is at last fulfilled'; the mistrust was apparent, even in the centre. Twelve deputies of the People's Party left the hall when Stresemann presented his cabinet to the Reichstag. In Bavaria he was nick-named 'Marxist' because he had made a coalition with the Social Democrats. But all that was mild enough, although it was meant maliciously. In the Fascist Press the tone was different. Significantly he was compared to Rathenau; he was accused of being 'the latest outpost of the sages of Zion', 'the little pet of the British and the French'.

Two men had fallen to the shots of Nationalist gangsters; the accusation that his complacency towards the Entente had been too great was equivalent to signing his death-warrant. The murders had happened before the advance of the French into the Ruhr. Since then the Ruhr war had become a great national undertaking which powerfully appealed to every patriotic instinct.

On September 26th the Stresemann government declared the cessation of passive resistance. That made it possible for the industrialists to make agreements with the Allied Control Commission, the so-called Micum agreements. Poincaré now had what he wanted and what the Germans had so long refused, 'productive pledges, territorially defined', in a part of Germany which already was half torn from her. The attempt to secure an agreement by diplomatic means had failed. Britain refused to take any steps thereto, the psychological moment was held to have passed. France neither released the prisoners nor allowed the expelled to return. In vain had the Chancellor in his Stuttgart speech and again, ten days later, in Berlin taken up the idea of 'productive pledges', offered mortgages on railways, industry, landed estates, all capable of being pledged—but in an unpartitioned Germany. Now something more definite than the mere prospect of payments weighed with the French. The weekly Sunday speeches of the French Premier were a nasty answer, and in every issue the *Temps* announced that the Stresemann cabinet was a failure and ought to disappear.

In a proclamation which the President and the Government of the Republic issued, the truth was revealed to the public. One hundred thousand Germans had been expelled from hearth and home. over a hundred had been killed, hundreds were in the prisons of a foreign soldiery. But in the last weeks the subsidies had reached a total of three and a half billion marks. 'We are faced with the bitter necessity of breaking off the fight.' This was capitulation; all Germany and the world should know it. As a rule it is a characteristic of commanders to keep silent about defeats; this commander-in-chief refused to gloss over the realities of the situation.

The mainspring of Stresemann's policy was national sentiment, even nationalist sentiment. He had once said of himself that two souls dwelt in him, one national and the other liberal, and so all his impulses were exaggerated. At one moment he was ultra-national, at another ultra-liberal. The study of his past career lets one see that the first was stronger than the second. Not only national but nationalist—that had been his attitude before and during the war. He was in the main stream of German imperialism until the war came. Fleets, colonies, world-trade, German expansion, were his favourite themes. In the war he supported the Army Command at all costs, took up every idea of conquest and expansion, shared the aims of the Fatherland Party. He greeted with joy unrestricted U-boat warfare. Now, at last, America would enter the enemy coalition. The mines of Briey and Longwy, Flanders, the Baltic lands, he wished to bring into the Empire. And if Calais was there for the winning, why, he asked, should not one win it? Ever and again he invoked Ulrich von Hutten: 'I repent, I strew ashes on my head, because I did not have stouter faith in victory.'

When defeat came he cursed the disarmament. He dreamed of an army of one hundred thousand men which could have made the Peace Treaty different. 'Even if all the deserters had fled away, what was left of the army would have prevented the humiliation of the Empire.' The Rhine would have held the victors at bay. He thought that the German river was an impregnable barrier. He was never tired of recalling Hannibal, who reproached the Punic Senate with the disarmament of Carthage: 'Then, then should ye have wept. . . .'

If national feeling had blinded him in these earlier days, now it made his vision keener. When all around him was in a state of collapse, he stood erect. Without and within the situation was horrible, hopeless; a worse could not be imagined. But in his speech on assuming office the Chancellor said with full confidence that things were not absolutely desperate. For a people which possessed strength of purpose the difficulties did not seem to be insuperable. To those who heard him it seemed that the new leader of the Republic spoke lightly, even frivolously. He believed in the nation which he loved. In spite of all the horror, a belief not founded on reason gave him certainty. It gave him strength to turn his eyes to far horizons. Romance seized on him again, but it is another sort of romance. It permitted him now to carry out the realist policy that the hour demanded. Nothing but that enabled him to rise superior to the political tasks of the day. While he bent all his energies against the obstacles which lay in his path, there remained before him a goal of light which gleamed on the horizon.

There were not a few politicians who were convinced that the Rhineland must be, at least temporarily, surrendered. I do not mean the cohorts of separatists, fools and poor devils, who for a couple of francs, for food and clothing, were ready to play the traitor and here and there, at the bidding of a French officer, cry out for a 'Rhenish Republic'. I mean those very agreeable and respectable gentlemen who feared that Poincaré's insistence on 'territorially defined productive pledges' was irresistible. For a time, until a new world situation arose, perhaps a new war, the Rhineland would have to suffer some sort of separation. When such opinions were voiced at a conference at Hagen, Stresemann's face flushed angrily and the debate—he could be very unpleasant—became bitter. Such things should not be said in his, the German Chancellor's, presence. The mutilation of Germany even if there was a cunning policy hidden behind the idea of it, he declared he could not stomach.

The surrender in the Ruhr was a national humiliation. In passionate speeches that could be denied, but it was so all the same. So great had the drama of the passive resistance been, so great had been its effect on Germany and on the world—to give it up was a moment of sorrow and shame for the nation.

The *Kreuzzeitung* asked in scornful bitterness if the Chancellor's dream had come true now. He had indeed dreamed dreams of national glory when in the tiny room he had sat buried in Treitschke's *History of Germany*: dreams of glory; and now the moment of the nation's greatest shame had come.

Scheidemann had said that the hand that signed the Peace Treaty would wither, and had won tumultuous applause. Stinnes had been congratulated when, at the international coal conference at Spa, he had struck the table with his clenched fist. The Foreign Minister, Simons, after he had said 'No' in London, had been greeted by wildly cheering crowds at the Lehrter station. The elegant general manager Cuno, when he unchained the Ruhr resistance, had been hailed as a hero. Stresemann knew, as every one knew, by what methods easy glory is won. But because he believed that in the end no difficulty could not be overcome by the German people, therefore he led it through the Caudine forks of capitulation. Before he issued that Government proclamation by which passive resistance was abandoned did he hesitate? We do not know. Did he think of resignation? He too could strike tables with his clenched fist, he too could say 'No' as others had done; he could resign his post, he could shuffle off responsibility, he could appear before the nation with a flaming appeal, he could declare that so disgraceful an order might be possible for others but never for him, he could have drawn down upon himself that storm of national applause which is so sweet and satisfying, he could have kept his prestige unimpaired for future deeds, for future honours. He did none of these things. He took upon himself what was inevitable, what the nation had to endure.

Before these days Stresemann had ever and anon played a brilliant part in political life. Later he won successes, gained distinctions. His great hour came when he stopped the Ruhr war.

The Stresemann cabinet, which had been formed on August 12th, in a day, in a few hours of conferences between the party leaders and founded on a rare enough agreement of political ideas, was brought down on October 23rd. It was reconstructed with some trouble without the Minister of Finance, Hilferding, and the Minister of the Treasury, von Raumer. On November 2nd the Social Democratic Ministers withdrew; it held on as a rump cabinet, but fell finally on November 23rd. The Great Coalition therewith came to an end for the moment.

In these few weeks—once again Germany had had a cabinet of a hundred days—political work had been accomplished such as in other circumstances is not accomplished in years. The economic collapse, the bankruptcy of the national finances, revolution and counter-revolution made most difficult decisions necessary.

In Saxony the local government was under Communist influence; the summoning of a works councils' congress showed the tendency to the Bolshevik ideal. The workers armed themselves. They armed themselves against an invasion which threatened to come out of Bavaria. In North Bavarian Coburg, Captain Ehrhardt, the military leader of the Kapp 'putsch', was assembling volunteer corps fully equipped with all the weapons of modern war. The Saxon Premier Zeigner in public fiercely attacked the Reichswehr Minister. The commander of the Bavarian Division, General von Lossow, rebelled, and with his troops passed into the service of and took the oath to Bavaria. The High Commissioner of the Bavarian State, von Kahr, abetted this act of high treason.

Saxony was directly dealt with by the national Government. Troops invaded her territory, and Heinze, the People's Party deputy, was sent to Dresden as commissioner of the national Government. Thuringia, too, which had entered into a close alliance with Saxony, was occupied. The Chancellor would have been quite prepared to send troops into Bavaria as well. Such an act was quite in keeping with his feeling for the honour of the nation. But he did not force things so far. The Government contented itself with protests. In the night of November 8th to 9th Hitler in the Munich Bürgerbrau declared the President of the Republic and the national Government deposed, placed the 'German National Army' under General Ludendorff, and issued a decree: 'I assume the direction of national policy.' Then broke out the conflict between the black, red, and white flag of the Empire and the white and blue of Bavaria, and the Bavarian front broke in two. The particularist von Kahr, partisan of the Wittelsbacher, gained the upper hand. Hitler fled and 'the national revolution' which was to have come out of Bavaria miscarried.

The different treatment applied to these two States was not a question of justice; it was not based on legality. It was possible to use force against Saxony; Bavaria was too strong. But by the occupation of Central Germany the national troops were placed directly in the path of Ehrhardt's threatening columns. Their movement to the north was made impossible. Not what was just, but what was necessary was done. It was also what was clever. Foreign policy, the surrender on the Ruhr, the resumption of reparations negotiations—all that was far more important than events inside Germany. The foe of Stresemann's foreign policy was the Right. The defeat of Saxony to the Right was something positive. Heinze's mission bound the right wing of the People's Party to the Government. Stresemann did yet another thing which could not fail to please the Right. He allowed the Crown Prince to return to Germany. That was taking a risk as far as the Entente was concerned. He took the responsibility for the risk. He explained to the British Ambassador that Wirth had already granted the Prince permission to return and that the Social Democratic Ministers must willy-nilly agree. But the act was quite in keeping with Stresemann's liberal policy that no German should be exiled from his Fatherland, and finally with the sympathy which he had always had with the sporting figure of this scion of the House of Hohenzollern.

In the revolution and inflation periods the number of officials had increased in an amazing fashion. The Stresemann government got the law passed reducing their numbers. Production had to be increased and the Stresemann government repealed the law establishing the eight-hour day. The dismissed officials were bitter; the workers seeing the greatest victory of the revolution brought to naught shook their fists.

But all these political labours of Hercules were put in the shade by the labour to create a new currency. Was the Rentenmark nearer the proposals of the Nationalist deputy Helfferich, the ex-Secretary of the Treasury, or to those of the Democratic bank director Schacht, who since November 11th had been Currency Commissioner? How much had the ideas of the Social Democrat Finance Minister Hilferding to do with it? That does not concern the real importance of the event. The National Government, the Stresemann Cabinet, carried out the return to the gold standard. The interest in the currency depreciation from which not only the much-abused speculators on 'change but also very respectable industrialists had reaped considerable profits, now disappeared. This was the 'miracle of the Rentenmark', a miracle which occurred in the Chancellorship of Gustav Stresemann.

Simultaneously with the cessation of passive resistance a state of siege was declared and plenipotentiary powers were conferred on the Reichswehr Minister. From a legal point of view Germany was under a military dictatorship. The generals held full sway over the life of the people, they could order as they pleased. In German history they have not seldom, though without such extraordinary powers, lorded it over a black-coated government. This time they remained, as befitted them, the policemen of the civil power. There was not lacking an attempt on the part of the generals to substitute themselves for that Government. Once before Stresemann had encountered such tendencies, and then he had done his utmost to make the Army Command all-powerful. But then the Chancellor had been Bethmann-

Hollweg. To-day he was the Chancellor. He had no ambition 'to run around with streaming eyes' whining about military encroachments. And so the encroachments never came to anything.

From another side the idea of dictatorship was presented to Stresemann. In the first half of November the leader of the Stahlhelm, Seldte, was three times received by the Chancellor. His visits were a sad disillusionment for him. In a report he admits: 'I got the impression that the present Chancellor was not the man to screw up sufficient resolution to be head of a national dictatorship as well as the national, and in the last resort, the Prussian government.' Before demands like the dissolution of the Reichstag, the kicking out of the Socialists from the Prussian Government, ruthless introduction and most rapid solution of the currency problem and of the food question the Chancellor retreated. There was a draft of a scheme for a directory circulating among the Stahlhelm in which Stresemann was to be 'Director of Foreign Policy', and was 'to wind up the parliamentary system'. What the leader of the Stahlhelm calls retreat one prefers to regard as a firm stand on his own line. But that Stresemann in those difficult circumstances should find time to receive Herr Seldte three times shows how greatly he exerted himself to keep in close touch with every quarter where he felt there might exist reserves of national strength. And he knew just where his chief enemy would be found.

In these 'hundred days' of chaotic happenings there were many minor incidents. The 'Black Reichswehr' risked their 'putsch'. The Palatinate separated from Bavaria and set up a republic of its own. It is impossible to enumerate how many things each of which in other circumstances would have been a catastrophe the Chancellor had to overcome, and did overcome. He acquired the habit of having the conference in which he always delighted at midnight or at two in the morning, although by eight o'clock he was at the telephone. But his working day—one of twenty hours—seemed really to have no limits in time. And just as limitless was the sphere of that work. He carried on before the world the great debate with Poincaré, who never spoke with Germany more harshly or more inexorably. He negotiated personally with the Bavarian, the Saxon, the Württemberg Premier. In an exchange of notes in the grand style with the Munich Cardinal Faulhaber he appealed to the prince of the Church to co-operate in the salvation of the State. He spoke not only in Berlin but in many other places at mass meetings. No warning prevented him going to explain his policy. Not for a moment did he cease to pay attention to the Press. He worked breathlessly, yet without ever losing his poise, and did what ten men could not have done. No banker would have risked one hundred thousand dollars on Germany's surviving. But the Chancellor defended his country tooth and nail. Revolution and counter-revolution, separatism, every sort of hostility to the State was experienced every day. At any moment the end might come. He looked the danger in the face, met it, averted it. While Germany seemed nearer death than life, the laws were passed which should restore the dying State to health.

Two lines ran counter to one another. The State was sinking, falling into the abyss. The Chancellor, who had flung himself as a barrier against the downward movement, grew, in certainty of feeling and of touch, in reputation before men, in the cabinet, to all who in amazement watched him working as if he was a thousand horse-powered machine, and who understood him and his historic significance.

In his own party there appeared signs of decomposition. The Bavarian group seceded, and inside the Parliamentary Party there was created a 'National Liberal League' which later seceded to the Nationalists.

But for the moment the Left bore the heaviest burdens. The conference of full powers on the military, the return of the Crown Prince, the abolition of the eight-hour day, above all the crushing by force of Socialist Central Germany caused the confidence of the worker in Social Democracy to dwindle to a dangerous extent. The party could no longer disregard the warnings. Already on November 2nd its Ministers had left the Cabinet.

The Chancellor recognized the growing opposition to him both on Left and Right. But he had accomplished a great work, and so was still, and even to the last, of good courage. On November 22nd Lord d'Abernon dined with him. He reports: 'Stresemann was dead tired, but revived somewhat under the influence of champagne.' Full of optimism, he told the Ambassador that the prospects of his cabinet surviving had considerably improved in the last forty-eight hours. He doubted if the Social Democrats would vote unanimously against him. He hoped that at next day's session he would defeat the opposition. In recalling that evening the English diarist half sceptically, half admiringly says:

'Stresemann is so confident in his own power that he thinks nothing is impossible.'

On November 23rd the Social Democratic Party voted with the Nationalists against the Government. The Stresemann cabinet was finally overthrown. When after such gigantic labour he sought some spot where he might win fresh strength, he could not find it in Germany. 'I can't go to Bavaria, for there they will have to protect me against the Hitler crowd. I can't go to Dresden or Thuringia, for there they will have to protect me against the Communists.' In the neighbourhood of Berlin he feared acquaintances would use every pretext to visit him to obtain his views on the fate of the Rentenmark. In the end he went to the Italian lakes; here he hoped it would be cold enough to let him have peace.

With the surrender in the Ruhr war, Stresemann definitely chose his path. The call of romance might have led him to others. When he did what was necessary in a spirit of realism he lost all round. He laid the foundation of his national and international reputation. He had to pay for it in great loss of popularity. He resigned the Chancellorship and a Marx cabinet in which he was Foreign Minister replaced his ministry. At the Reichstag elections which took place on May 5th came the reckoning. His own party lost a third of their seats. The Social Democrats lost three-sevenths of theirs. The Democrats suffered very heavily. The Nationalists, with one hundred members, were the strongest party in Parliament. To the right of them sat thirty-six Fascists and on the extreme left sixty-two Communists.

CHAPTER VII

THE POLICY OF 'AS IF'

IT was the general opinion that it would be as foolish as it would be useless to restore the currency before the reparations problem was solved. To act as if that vital question did not exist and to make policy independent of it—that may have been demanded by individuals but was rejected by the majority. All that Stresemann had done as Chancellor was under the influence of terrible pressure, exercised by the precipitous fall in the currency. When passive resistance was abandoned, the dollar in one week rose from one hundred and thirty million to six hundred million marks. When the Zeigner government of the proletariat came into power in Saxony it rose from three milliards to five, and when the Bavarian division rebelled, from twelve milliards to forty. Just before the issue of the Rentenmark the dollar in one day rose by half its value and on another by double that. On November 20th, three days before the fall of the cabinet, the exchange was stable. When the Stresemann cabinet resigned, the chaos of depreciation was over. Quiet reigned on 'change. The mark did not oscillate again. There is no standard by which we can measure the loss in energy, in force, in vitality which the fluctuations of the currency cost.

The stability of the currency was completed ; the solution of the reparations problem lay completely in the unknown. That was a contradiction of the ruling thesis; still more of the systematic thought of the Germans. First the definite fixing of the compensations to be paid and the yearly sums to be handed over, then the levying of the necessary taxes, then a balanced budget, and then as a final victory the stabilization of the currency. Orderly thinkers could not imagine events in any other sequence. It was not easy for Germany to get accustomed to the apparently desultory and idiotic policy of putting the cart before the horse. Now necessity had smashed the sequence of orderly thinkers; the necessary policy had triumphed. Again one could reckon with fixed values, as if the budget was balanced, as if the annual payments to the victors had been fixed.

The event is a symbol of all that is to happen later. No other nation had been so accustomed as Germany to reckon things political by values state-able in figures, to compare nations, for instance, by their areas in square miles, by their inhabitants by the million, by their position in the world in terms of the size of their armies, the number of their guns and ships. This military method is the most obvious; it is therefore the point round which thought turns. That is why disarmament was so particularly pain-ful, so intolerable. The army of one hundred thousand men was nothing compared to the huge armies of neighbours, great and small. Strength which exists only potentially was unkind consolation for us. That is why no one in Germany can ever understand why France trembles for her security. In France people think of what has been and what might be again. In Germany people think in just the opposite way. When the French politicians declare that their land can be threatened that seems to Germany a lie, a mockery.

The policy which had to be carved out after 1923 led directly away from the usual practice of thought. Germany was compelled to stop reckoning in figures, to cease estimating effective strengths, if it desired again to become a subject of international negotiations; the German nation had to think in terms of achievements and qualities for which there is no material standard of reckoning if it wished to recover its self-esteem. That was a difficult reversing process and constituted a far profounder revolution than the political one. To all it was difficult, to many impossible. Every day it was made more difficult because Germany's former enemies had devoted themselves to reckoning up with painful thoroughness her soldiers, her policemen, her rifles. The bureaucratic pen-pusher is a military speciality, and on the other side had become a very important person after the victory of the soldiers. Their words were much better understood in Germany than the voices of reconciliation which came over one by one from the enemy camp. But the inner reversal did what was needed. We had to conduct policy as if our sovereignty were unimpaired.

The leader along this rocky path was Stresemann. The conversion which the German people completed panting and gasping he had first to experience in his own individual case. He started with the same sort of thinking, the same sort of self-estimation as all Germany. He too had clung to the primitive conception of power much more ardently than had the majority of his countrymen. Had he not violently reproached Kühlmann because that Secretary of State wished to trust to political effort to secure an end to the war? Only one thing, according to Stresemann, could bring peace to the world: 'Not the speeches of statesmen, not diplomatic negotiations, no diplomatic notes, no Reichstag resolutions, but the hammer of Ludendorff, the strength of our army, the power of our armed might. . . .'

And at that same period he had given up the idea of a World League of Peace for the absurdity of the 'Independent Committee for a German Peace'.

'We have had once already experience of such a world league. . . . Abandoned just as the German Emperor was on the field of lies of Algeciras. . . . We would be abandoned again if Germany's future were to be settled under neutral presidency. . . .'

Now he himself consented to put Germany's fate before conferences for decision, to lead Germany into a World League of Peace. To no one more than to him was the thought more foreign that spirit and personality brought to a conference could achieve as much as strong battalions on the battle-field. To be sure, at that time men in whom he had very little confidence would have had the handling of negotiations. Now he himself was in charge of affairs. And as no other way to Germany's recovery stood open, his eyes were open now to the other possibilities he had ignored. It is the spark of genius which at the right moment brings him the new knowledge.

Despite her defeat, despite her disarmament, Germany has remained one of the great European nations. Whoever seeks to lead her must conduct affairs as if his country had not been defeated, had not been disarmed. The Treaty of Versailles had condemned us to payments whose burden must be borne. The obligation thereto exists, rests not on moral guilt but simply on the fact that our adversaries were stronger. If we fulfil the treaty we enjoy equal rights and privileges ; then it is as if the treaty were really a treaty and not an imposition.

A state of the area, population, and length of frontier of Germany cannot be defended according to the old conceptions by so tiny an army as is left us. Round about her stand greater armies, and so by the standard of numbers she is defenceless. That is the usual conception. Germany had to act as if her frontiers were not threatened.

From the stabilization of the currency, as if the reparations total had been fixed, in trade treaty negotiations, in economic congresses, in inter-parliamentary conferences, disarmament discussions, sports meetings, right up to the entry of Germany into the League of Nations, it is everywhere a case of the policy of 'as if'. For any nation the carrying out of an 'as if' policy is difficult, but most difficult of all for the German. The politician who realized most completely its possibilities was Stresemann. He was the first to make it peculiarly his own.

There were four stages on the rocky way—the Dawes Plan, Locarno, Germany's entry into the League of Nations, the Hague Conference. Even then the rocky path had not reached its end, but Stresemann's life had. One goal had been reached, though only a preliminary goal, but still a goal which at the beginning had seemed scarcely possible to reach, which promised the nation a great moment of pride ; he sees before him—the liberation of the Rhineland. Then he sinks back ; it is finished.

The process began when an international committee of experts met in Berlin to examine the state of Germany's finances. The American banker Dawes was its chairman. That was the beginning of the beginning of the retreat to the ways of reason. The committee demanded that the economic unity of Germany be restored. Otherwise there was no need to expect reparations. In this conception there was no place for the favourite idea of Poincaré, 'territorially defined productive pledges'. France appeared to be delaying. Then the French nation withdrew its confidence from the *Bloc national*. Herriot of the Radical Socialist Party succeeded Poincaré. Stresemann heard the news at Karlsruhe. In an interview he spoke of silver rays on the horizon. In Britain the first Labour Government came into power. A new springtime of the peoples seemed to be warming the earth. For the disagreements which in late years had divided the two great allied nations, Germany had always had to pay the bill. When MacDonald received Herriot at Chequers and, sitting like a boy with him on the grass, spoke about Europe, cordial relations were restored between the two States. Germany came to London. The new Chancellor Marx, the leader of the Catholic Centrists, a sound lawyer, Stresemann and the Finance Minister Luther, formerly Burgomaster of Essen, were her representatives. MacDonald called the conference 'the first true peace conference'.

It certainly was the first peace conference in the sense that things were discussed and negotiated, and that it was not just a case of giving and receiving dictatorial commands. The basis of its being so, however, was the extreme spirit of self-sacrifice with

AN ANXIOUS LEAGUE DISCUSSION

A PHOTOGRAPH TAKEN AT LUGANO IN DECEMBER 1928

Left to right: M. Zaleski (Polish Foreign Minister), Sir Austen Chamberlain, Herr Stresemann, Signor Scialoja (Italian Council Member), M. Briand

which Germany gave up the passive resistance and the self-control which was revealed by that sacrifice of a resistance which it took more heroism to end than to begin.

Germany was then in principle once again unpartitioned. Efforts therefore were made in London to secure that foreign troops would leave the territories they had occupied. The one thing was gained, but not the other. The French contention that the period within which evacuation had to be made had not yet begun because Germany was not yet fulfilling her treaty obligations—a theory by which the occupation could last an indefinite time—was no longer pressed. German sovereignty was to be restored; those condemned during the Ruhr war were to be released, Germany's legal authority be re-established, the expelled to be allowed to return. Evacuation was what Stresemann had at heart. His feelings were outraged by the presence of foreign rule on German soil. That it should cease was not just so clear then as it was five years later. A party friend of the Minister's, a Rhinelander in a high political position, asked him sceptically: 'Do you really believe that the French will ever leave the Ruhr?' And Herriot, hard pressed in London, had cried: 'Without the Ruhr I dare not go back to Paris.' Stresemann kept on pressing. What was happening did not please him. Evacuation kept being put off till the August of next year. Every town had to be fought for. Dortmund and Hörde would be evacuated when the Dawes plan was accepted as a sort of prepayment on account of liberation.

A plan of payment was accepted by which Germany should receive a moratorium and a loan

and then should pay sums of increasing amounts in a normal year, two and a half milliards of marks—a figure which was the result of negotiations and not a mere imposition. That was an important point. Still more important was the fact that it was made possible to retain the amounts in the country if the German currency was threatened, and further, to have them decreased. The number of the yearly payments was not fixed.

In Germany the obligation under the Dawes Plan was considered high—intolerably high. But it was not an iron obligation ; it was not unalterable. Once Germany had found insecurity, uncertainty the worst burden of all. Now she found it to be a factor which could be used in favour of the vanquished. The victors had become exasperated ; nothing had ever been done to allay that bitterness. Therefore the demands could really not be estimated by ordinary standards. Only slowly could a standard be found. Always to have the last step left in doubt and darkness—that had seemed to the untutored Germans as the worst of dangers. Now they had to learn to see in it good fortune ; to educate a democratically organized people, and one so inexperienced in democracy, to such a policy as it had formerly shrunk from was a toilsome effort and demanded the highest art.

Herriot was welcomed in Paris by crowds of cheering adherents. '*Vive la paix !*' the crowd shouted, tired of the quarrel between the allies, tired of moral isolation.

The German Ministers had no such reception awaiting them. As long as Germany was compelled only to admissions, so long as she received her burdens under protest, so long the people could hope in the help of Heaven, could endure catastrophes, each new woe appearing to conceal within it a promise of redemption. Now it was a question of bestirring oneself to take up a voluntary burden, to endure the consequences of a defeat that had never been quite admitted. The desperate rebelliousness of the past years had been romance, if the romance of agony. It was now time to be not merely diplomatic, but positively practical. The leader to this change was one who himself had willingly dreamed so many romantic dreams and who only with difficulty turned to reality—Stresemann.

The task which the Minister undertook was difficult enough—to get the Reichstag to agree to the Dawes Plan. The middle-class parties represented only a minority in Parliament. They could count on their own members and equally on the Social Democrats. But one of the Dawes laws—the law on the mortgage of the State railways—meant an amendment of the Constitution. Such an amendment requires a two-thirds majority, and so the law could not be carried against the united opposition of the Nationalists. That was not just a merely formal obstacle. It was also highly desirable that nothing should be done completely without and against the Nationalists. The work of peace without them would be very insecure and of no great value. A motion to declare that the State Railways Bill did not constitute an amendment to the Constitution was defeated. Already in London the Government had committed themselves to that two-thirds majority. In the lobbies of the Reichstag, which once he had angrily called 'cynical', but which he ruled as an instrument with sovereign power, there never was such excited negotiating as in these days of extreme tension, in which once again, as it had been so often in this period of history, part of Germany's, part of Europe's destiny was at stake. The President of the Republic had determined to dissolve the Reichstag if the Dawes Bills were not passed. Possibly it would have been possible to defeat the Nationalists and the extreme parties, whose policy was simply blank negation, and after the election one could have the necessary two-thirds majority for the Dawes Bills. But that was not what Stresemann wanted.

A policy of fulfilment had once before been adopted by the Wirth cabinet, which had thrown down the challenge to the Nationalists : ' The enemy is on the right.' Stresemann had now begun to conduct a policy of fulfilment, but it was a ' policy of national realism ', as he preferred to call it. Wherein lay the difference ? Without sarcasm one may say : Only in words. The division into the two Germanys, *les deux Allemagnes* which they talked about in France, that was what the Minister would not have. He put forth a version of his own, in a phrase which a Paris paper had already coined—that there were ' three Germanys : the Germany of the Nationalists, the Germany of the Left Coalition, and the Germany of the People's Party '. He could without presumption have said that this third Germany of the synthesis was his own, was Stresemann's Germany.

Berlin wit likened him to the traffic policeman who stands on the control tower in the Potsdamer Platz ; he looks now right, now left, and every two minutes changes his colour. Was the comparison meant to disparage? Perhaps. Yet it is possible to take it as a compliment.

The United Fatherland Associations passed a threatening resolution—the London agreement must be rejected. It meant an enslavement of Germany. It was the habit of these associations to throw fine phrases into the party strife. But their close organization is the ideal of many Germans; threads go from them to the Nationalists, even to the People's Party, and these threads are many and strong. Would the Nationalist Party in Parliament cut themselves free of these threads? Two Germanys—that is the old Imperial Germany and the Germany of the black, red, and gold flags—Stresemann would not admit the division. His policy of national realism was the foreign policy of the Democrats and Social Democrats, so he made trial of them first. But he did not therefore belong to the new Germany; he felt far more in sympathy with the old. He repudiated the policy of his allies and said: 'It is not a matter of ascertaining the dividing line between the old Germany and the new; it is a matter of building a bridge from the one to the other.' The bridge was still unbuilt; only a temporary footway spanned the gulf; on left and right men sought to tear it down. It had one single defender, Stresemann.

In the lobbies they haggled and haggled. The great decision which the nation had to take upon itself was here being negotiated in small change. Personal considerations had already played a part which was to be important in the future. They have always played too great a part in the history of the young German parliamentaryism. Finally, on

August 28th a letter went from the deputies of the People's Party to the Nationalist Parliamentary Party. The People's Party will 'support by all the means in its power the participation of the Nationalists in the Government in numbers proportionate to their importance'.

On August 30th signature had to take place in London. Only one day more. On that day the hundred deputies of the Nationalist Party split. Fifty-two maintained their negative; forty-eight voted with the Government. The Dawes Plan was saved.

The Chancellor was desirous of broadening the basis of the coalition. He paid court to Left and Right, but got no affection in return. Ebert dissolved the Reichstag. The last elections had been 'catastrophe elections'; the electors had been under the influence of inflation, the Ruhr war, and starvation. Now an improvement in the parliamentary situation might be hoped for. December 7th was election day. The extreme parties were beaten. The Fascists again became only an unimportant group; the Communists lost seventeen seats. The centre parties held their ground. But the People's Party, the party of the Foreign Minister Stresemann, did not recover its strength. In the first Reichstag it had been sixty-five strong, only one less in numbers than the Nationalists. The Right, which, except for that one compliance, had always stood fast on its platform of negation, shot ahead of them. It held one hundred and eleven seats. But as the Socialists had partly regained lost seats they were the strongest party in the Reichstag—with one hundred and thirty-one deputies. To get a majority together was just as difficult as it had been before. Ebert entrusted

Stresemann with the task of cabinet-building. But as the Centrists would not join a Government in which the Right shared, and the People's Party rejected alike the Great Coalition and a minority Government he gave up the attempt.

This was the first of the Christmas crises which have become a tradition in Germany. It lasted thirty-nine days. The Press of the Left fiercely attacked Stresemann because he stood stubbornly for the entry of the Nationalists into the Government. He recommended as Chancellor the former Finance Minister Luther, who had been with him in London, and was of Conservative leanings but without party-affiliations. On January 19th Luther presented his cabinet to the Reichstag. It was composed mainly of experts. The Right had so constantly appealed for them that, for once, an experiment was made with them. The Nationalists, Centrists, and Bavarian People's Party had each a man of confidence in the Ministry. That Stresemann remained as Foreign Minister goes without saying. What the Chancellor had to say on the question of the Constitution was this: 'The legal basis for the work of this Government is the Republican Constitution of August 11, 1919.' One can hardly call this a generous acknowledgement of the Republic. His foreign political programme affirmed the London agreement and in principle the entry of Germany into the League of Nations. With that the Left agreed. The Social Democrat Breitscheid said in his speech on the Government's statement of policy: 'I feared that the mission of the Foreign Minister to convert the Nationalists would end in his own conversion.'

Stresemann was not ‘ converted ’. On February 9, 1925, by order of the Government, a note was handed to the Allies whose contents for the moment were kept a profound secret. Different possibilities were envisaged in it. The Rhine States, with Britain and Italy, could pledge troth to the United States never to wage war one against the other. They might also guarantee the territorial *status quo* on the Rhine. That was nothing less than an offer to conclude peace—a real peace. The Peace of Versailles was not a peace at all. The London agreement was only the outline of one. So long as a policy of fulfilment consisted only in complacencies it never produces anything but refusals. Now Germany had seized the initiative. How clever the initiative was Lord d'Abernon has plainly told us. Had the note become known, he says, there is ‘ scarcely any doubt but that Stresemann would have been compelled to resign, and it is even highly probable that he would have fallen victim to an outrage ’. The circle of those who knew of it was very small ; the Nationalist man of confidence in the cabinet later was able to say truthfully that he knew nothing about the note.

Cuno had once before made a somewhat similar offer but no one either at home or abroad had trusted him. Nor was it really similar. He had only offered a temporary peace. And not only is a thing not the same thing when two do it. It is equally not the same when it is done at a different time. Even now it comes early. The horrors of the Ruhr war have been over for little more than a year. But the plans which many Frenchmen designed for the Rhineland have been given up. The European situation is favourable. Yet it was a clever stroke of policy, both of home and foreign policy, that Stresemann had made. It was the continuation of the policy of 'as if' which was so new for Germany and which now, to the astonishment of Europe, was conducted so magisterially at the Wilhelmstrasse. Negotiations would take place as if the sacrosanct Treaty of Versailles were not thereby being upset, as if there were no great obstacles to the entry of Germany into the League of Nations, as if no wide tracts of German territory were occupied, as if a reparations total had been fixed. A spirit of high adventure strode over all obstacles.

Was it Stresemann who did all that? Later there was controversy on the point. Once, when the new policy did not seem to be going well, others had no desire to take any credit for the brilliant initiative. Stresemann was ready to take sole responsibility for it. Then when things began to go well again, others made their claims. But this dispute about credit, which had no political significance, left Stresemann cold. He could have established his title, but did not trouble. The generations to come will recognize him as the only begetter of the policy and will be right.

The note was received in a friendly spirit. In August, France invited the Germans to oral negotiations. On October 5th the statesmen met at Locarno. Herriot and MacDonald were no longer in power. For France Aristide Briand came, for Britain Austen Chamberlain. Germany was represented by Luther, the Chancellor, and by Stresemann. When they left Berlin the police had to take special precautions for their safety.

This was the time when the world began to sit

up and take notice of the German Foreign Minister—in October 1925—only four years before his death, when it hailed him as a great European and a great peacemaker. Up to this time it knew little about him. What had he done to win men's confidence? The German Social Democrats in the past years had been the only party in Germany to maintain some sort of international connexions. They recommended Stresemann to their French comrades and to the Belgian Social Democrat, Vandervelde, who as Foreign Minister represented his country at Locarno. 'Suspect in home politics,' they said, thinking from a party point of view, 'for international understanding absolutely trustworthy.' Then too a French Socialist who played some part in foreign politics, the deputy Grumbach, had also conceived this opinion of him. That happened in April 1923, when the Ruhr war was at its fiercest. French, Belgian, British, and Italian Socialists had met with German Socialists in Berlin, and Grumbach had sought out the leader of the People's Party to discuss with him the possibility of reconciliation. The conversation had no practical result. Poincaré would not yield, and Cuno could find no way out. But the deputy Stresemann said to the Frenchman: 'If we do not learn to understand each other, you and we, we are lost both of us and Europe with us.' Grumbach had never forgotten the passionate earnestness with which these words were spoken.

The world which ran excitedly after this new man of note about whom it knew so little, what did it see? An English journalist later set down definitely the impression which Stresemann made. He said: 'Externally Stresemann is a typical German, even the typical caricature of a German, with his bullet head, close-cropped, almost bald, thick neck, ruddy cheeks, little eyes. He is vivacious and easily roused. His laughter is noisy. And then he is an astonishing eater and drinker. During a meal glass after glass of beer vanishes down his throat.'

What the English observer saw was not really Stresemann's outward appearance. It was the mask under which ill-health was even then concealing him. Long before this the weak heart could only slowly supply blood to the powerful frame. No sports had been open to the boy from the Kopenicker Strasse; the army would not have him, and then came this life of desks and conference tables. When an English party leader arrives in the morning in a foreign capital, in the afternoon he is out with the ambassador pursuing a golf ball. Only in last years of his life was a vain attempt made at Oberhof to induce the German Foreign Minister to become acquainted with the mysteries of golf. Sport and the worship of it were alike hateful to him. He had no time, German that he was, for such recreations, and the 'beer evenings' which play such a part in the political life of Berlin are an unhealthy continuation of political work. So a fine-cut mouth and shapely nose soon disappeared beneath watery, bloated skin. The cheeks whose ruddiness was deceptive had compressed the expressive eyes; the ravages of his kidney trouble were plainly seen. But the hands revealed what Nature had intended in the beginning to make of him. The Englishman, who was a close observer, says: 'They were white, small, and delicate like those of a beautiful woman.' And the voice, clear, sharp, penetrating like a trumpet, which foreigners could not understand could belong to a German, at first rather grated on them than attracted. Disadvantages rather than advantages had Nature given him. In order to conquer he had to come out of himself. But his strength lay in this—that it came easy to him to overcome these obstacles, even in international negotiations which were new to him. People were accustomed to German diplomatists who were reserved and had concealed the man behind a uniform. Here was some one surprisingly different. It required only the shortest time for the German Foreign Minister to reveal the directness, the originality of his character. That was not only revealed in private conversations. He was recognized also as an orator. As his gift as a speaker did not rest on formal excellences but on the warmth and strength of his feeling, it failed him as little before ministers and their experts as before great public meetings. When he spoke men trusted him. This ' spirit of Locarno ', so much mentioned since the conference, too often with malicious irony, does not consist in a spirit of unlimited concession, in complacencies, but in that frankness with which anxieties and complaints were communicated to each other by the statesmen.

Chamberlain had been warned about the German Foreign Minister. Asquith had said to him : ' You don't know Stresemann ? Look at his photograph—a typical Junker. You won't find him easy.' The Englishman found the view correct. But gradually, so he tells us, he recognized how far Stresemann in character was from his conception of a ' Junker '.

In Locarno there began that close relationship between Briand and Stresemann which was so manifoldly and variously expressed. The old and experienced artist in politics spoke somewhat in this vein to his young German colleague : 'In my career I have won all the honours which I could wish. I have thoroughly tasted power and all its joys and sorrows. I have one ambition still, only one, to go down to history as the man who from the French side accomplished the reconciliation of our two countries.' Where Stresemann found confidence he gave it. He believed that Briand's words had but expressed his own feelings.

The version of the German Nationalists that Briand deluded Stresemann, made a fool of him, is without credibility. The Frenchman certainly was a magician, but the German was not the man to lose his clarity of vision under a spell. He remained firm where he neither could, nor wished to, change. In spite of French support at Locarno, the Polish aims at Locarno were not realized.

The converse was maintained and believed by the French Chauvinists. They said just what the German Nationalists were saying, but reversed the roles. In their story the German was the spell-binder. Observers who were close to events knew that conversations with Stresemann were not always a pleasure for Briand. The German Minister was persistent, untiring. Whenever one goal was reached, he was striving hard to the next. He was obstinate, he insisted. He was—and that made the situation historic—the one who had to make demands and he was never weary of demanding. But on these bases of frankness and insistence there developed between these two politicians a relation which was a more affectionate one than that which usually exists between diplomatic negotiators. When later they spoke of '*mein Freund,* Briand', '*Mon ami,* Stresemann', there was more in the phrases than mere politeness.

The Treaties of Locarno are characteristic results of the 'as if' policy. That France and Germany renounced ambitions, the recovery of Alsace on the one side and the annexation of the Rhineland on the other, was only a practical admission of reality. But that eternal peace had been declared on the Rhine while actually a state of war existed between the two States, that was for Germany a bold and brilliant negotiation. There was the occupied territory—first zone, second zone, third zone; there was the Saar basin; there were the restrictions on Germany's air development; there was disarmament—very many matters in which Germany was not equal in right but was under war necessity. The peace of Locarno was concluded as if agreement reigned everywhere, while actually no agreements had been made. The 'consequences' that Locarno should have were therefore not assured other than by the treaty itself, in which there was not a word said about them. It was about these consequences that Germany was especially anxious, and there was no lack of warning telegrams from the Ministers left behind in Berlin. What was required in the circumstances was romantic confidence in the man who saw all the happy results of his work of peace work themselves out before him, and a great self-confidence on the part of the man himself to believe that they would actually so develop. The man was Stresemann. The Chancellor Luther's part was simply to stand by and be of service. Both initialled the documents, although the cabinet by telegram asked for postponement. As is the diplomatic custom, they signed their initials and so personally assumed responsibility for the treaties. With music and illumination the little town on the blue lake celebrated the liberation of Europe as if it were really completed.

CHAPTER VIII

'A MARKED MAN'

ON February 28, 1925, the first President of the Republic, Friedrich Ebert, died. Against the candidature of Gessler the Reichswehr Minister, Stresemann successfully raised objections. Gessler's name had been too closely involved in the secret armaments scandal. The Foreign Minister feared that his election would be a blow to the policy of understanding.

Stresemann also tried to prevent the nomination of Field-Marshal von Hindenburg. A general as chief representative of Germany, that too might destroy the work which he had but begun. Opposition undoubtedly was not easy as for him. He honoured Hindenburg. He had shown that long ago and he was to show it again in years to come. Also this candidature was clearly the most promising. But foreign policy for which he was responsible was more to him than a party success, than personal sentiment. His romantic sense pled for the grey-haired commander-in-chief; practical considerations demanded that he prefer a burgomaster. He did not carry his point, but he made enemies.

When he returned from Locarno, he was fiercely assailed. At the Nationalist Party conference the 'policy of illusion' was 'branded'. A resolution said: 'The vital interests of Germany are not assured.' The Nationalist Minister, the man of confidence of the party and three non-party Ministers, the so-called experts, left the Government. The leader of the Nationalist Party in Parliament, Count Westarp, declared: 'So long as enemy troops are on German soil, we Germans live not in peace but in a state of war.'

In the Bavarian Parliament a Fascist deputy shouted: 'I could well understand an expelled Alsatian or Lorrainer shooting Stresemann at sight.'

On December 1st, after the Reichstag had approved the Locarno treaties, they were signed in London. On the same day the evacuation of the Cologne zone began. It was a slow business—very slow. Nothing in the world can move so slowly as a soldier when he sees no reason for haste.

In London congratulatory speeches were made. Briand said: 'I see in these treaties the renewal of Europe, the revelation of Europe's true character.' Stresemann said: 'If we go under we shall all go under together. We must not live in disunion and enmity. May it be that later generations will look back with gratitude to this day.'

A few months earlier, on the anniversary of Rathenau's murder, shots rang out in the garden of the Foreign Ministry. They were never explained.

In the *Preussische Landeszeitung* an ex-colonel compared Stresemann to a homicidal murderer or 'an equally useful member of society'. A Fascist paper was seized because it incited to violence against the Foreign Minister. On December 3rd a Nationalist ex-officer then employed in a Siemens factory wrote to a friend in Munich: 'I have made a rhyme after a well-known model, "Stresemann—corpse man". You understand? I have two officers to help me and the " financial side " is all right. The swine must be put away. An aeroplane also at our disposal.' The writer and an accomplice were arrested.

Stresemann's European policy had to be carried through without the Nationalists, and so again on a narrower parliamentary basis. After a Christmas crisis that lasted forty-five days, Luther formed a minority cabinet from the centre bourgeois parties. Count Westarp's speech in opposition to it began : ' From illusions to disillusionments, from disillusionments to new illusions : that is the hall-mark of the Stresemann policy. We want no new disillusionments for our Fatherland as a result of the entry of Germany into the League of Nations.' From illusions to disillusionments—the phrase seems very like the man of romance and realism. The tone, however, is very different. A Fascist deputy, a major on the retired list, spoke of ' the government of the servile jailers of their own people '.

Long ago, when he was Prime Minister, MacDonald at Geneva had alluded to ' the threatening aspect of the empty seats in our midst '. At Locarno, Germany had pledged herself to join the League of Nations, and in February sent in her formal request for admittance. The League members were invited to attend an extraordinary session which would be consecrated to the reception of the Republic. On March 5th Luther and Stresemann went to Geneva ; on March 17th they came back. The reception had not come off.

France and Britain had sought to give Poland a permanent seat on the Council simultaneously with Germany. Germany demanded that the composition of the Council should not be altered until she had been admitted to the League. China, Brazil, Spain equally wanted to join the Council. On the Sunday before the League session the Locarno Powers met in discussion. On Monday the French Government was overthrown and Briand hurried to Paris. Count Skrzynski, the Polish Foreign Minister, wished to yield. Briand hurried back and prevented him. Sweden and Czechoslovakia declared themselves ready to give up their seats on the Council to make room for the persistent candidates. Then Brazil declared that she would vote against Germany's admission. The play had been faultily staged; misunderstanding not malice prevented Germany from entering the League.

For eleven days Germany had waited at the gates of the League. The German delegates held fast to their standpoint. But what a triumph for the German Nationalist Press, for the politicians who had uttered warnings about the disillusionments which must follow illusions! Eleven days of a severe test of endurance; eleven days in which mental tension was such as to cause physical distress, in which Stresemann held conference after conference while splitting headaches racked him. Each morning it seemed as if a solution would be found; when evening came no solution had been reached. This entry into the League of Nations was to have come as the crown, as it were, of the work of peace; it was to signify that Germany had re-entered the great family of nations, it was to present to the world a sublime drama and one that was full of honour for Germany. What trouble, what toil, what risk had been taken! And now—what an end!

Not only the extreme Nationalists had warned and threatened, but far into the ranks of the centre men had doubted. What wealth of persuasion Stresemann had poured out upon his own party! And on each of the eleven days the falterers and the foes had called: 'Leave! Leave!' That would have meant a breach with the Locarno policy. But what a platform for home policy, for the next elections! For a demagogue, if the German Foreign Minister was one, what a chance! How the station in Berlin would have echoed with shouts of jubilant greeting if he turned his back on the Allies.

Emil Ludwig was in Geneva at the time. He showed plainly how disgusted the position of his country made him. When Stresemann asked him what he, the convinced pacifist, would do in such a case, he too said: 'Leave! Leave!' The Minister a hundred times abused for seeking only a personal satisfaction answered: 'The triumph is too cheap for me.'

It was Stresemann who held the position, who maintained himself by violent effort on the narrow ledge from which he wished to march upwards and onwards. It was Stresemann alone. The Chancellor, not very sure of the path which had not been his from the beginning weakened, had to be sustained instead of sustaining.

The German delegates waited till the end of the session. France and Britain demonstratively certified to them their own loyal handling of the situation. On their return to Berlin they received the Press. In these last excited days, Brazil, the disturber of the peace, had been bitterly criticized in the Press —even in that of the Left—had been vilified, insulted. There had been a certain joy taken in finding a whipping-boy in the distant land which, as far as Europe was concerned, was not a powerful State and was not considered quite civilized, and in making jests about the coco-nuts which these exotic folk had thrown at us from the tree-tops of their primeval forest. After the Chancellor had given a report, Stresemann took up the argument and sharply attacked this sort of polemic. This was the method which in pre-war days had made Germany so many enemies. Then the target for its shafts had been the Balkan States. To-day they were being aimed at South America. The men the sharp voice scolded were supporters of his policy. The Minister never thought of using the way of escape which had been prepared for him.

On April 24th the 'Treaty of Berlin' was signed, a treaty of neutrality between Germany and Russia. The West pricked up its ears and looked with suspicion to the German capital. Was this revenge for the disappointment at Geneva, a threat, perhaps a new orientation of German policy? It was nothing of the sort, and it was the Minister's duty to allay anxiety. His credit was good enough for that. Actually the new agreement was only a natural consequence of the Treaty of Rapallo, a necessary security in a situation which was still not without danger. Rapallo had been the result of the necessity felt to show the Allies that other ways were open to Germany. But this was 1926, not 1921. And Stresemann's character had none of the chameleon-like quality of Rathenau's, who loved to shine in many colours. Maltzan, at the time of Rapallo director of the Eastern Section of the Foreign Office, had since gone to be ambassador at Washington. Stresemann had insisted that he should be well out of the way. Lord d'Abernon thought that Locarno would never have happened if Maltzan had remained in Berlin. Actually, among the German politicians only those whose romanticism outstripped their sense of reality were adherents of the Russian orientation. Let us not speak of officers of the former Army Command, who thought it possible to combine an extremely Conservative position with the idea of the sacrifice of the West and the Bolshevization of the East—Germany was to be defended on the Elbe ! But Maltzan and Brockdorff-Rantzau, by nature aristocratic and unsympathetic to middle-class ideas, inclined to mysticism and spiritualism, who felt akin to Asia and the Russian soul, wished to move the centre of gravity to the East. Stresemann was very far from having such ideas. He was not at all pleased when the People's Commissary, Chicherin, announced his visit, regarded him as something strange, incomprehensible. He was a Westerner and loved clarity, reasonableness, the immediately attainable, the simple. Germany is on the way from East to West ; Stresemann, the leader of the nation, not its forerunner, goes with it. Karl Radek, but lately taken once again into favour by the Bolshevist clique, wrote in a scornfully sympathetic obituary notice of Stresemann that he was 'the representative of the interests of the German *bourgeoisie* ', and as such nothing much ; he was 'the representative of the transition period to a period of transition '. The Bolshevist rightly understood how far the German bourgeois stood from the Russian idea of life, an idea as vague as the vague limits of their limitless steppes. In the cult which he vowed to heroes, Stresemann never included the foreign name of Lenin. His romance was a matter of national sentiment. If always a sense of reality kept it in subjection and limited its vision, it was always love of country that was the guiding thought, contact with its past and with its future.

Some days after the German-Russian treaty was signed romance played him a trick, not the last it played him, but possibly the most dangerous. The President of the Republic issued a decree that took the whole nation by surprise. This was the famous 'flag orders'. Embassies and consulates in other continents and in Europe where merchant shipping touched, were from now on to fly both the merchant shipping flag and the black, red, and gold. Now, the merchants' shipping flag is the black, white, and red, with the national colours inserted, and each year the latter became smaller, ever more difficult to see. The double flag was a compromise, the most flagrant 'inconsequence' of the Constitution. A nation can have only one flag. The lack of unity in the German nation was demonstrated by this doubling, and was in turn kept in being by it. A decision had to be once and for all. And as it was the monarchists who displayed the black, white, and red as their party colours, it was a constitutional question that had to be decided simultaneously with the flag question. As late as 1924 the People's Party had resolved to dispense with the black, red, and gold. But two years is a long time when development goes on at such a speed.

The cabinet had authorized the orders before the President of the Republic issued them. Up rose at once a national storm. The most ticklish question from the point of view of national feeling had been raised. The Chancellor was an administrative expert, not a politician. He said much later that he did not understand really what had happened. But Stresemann, the man of political flair ' filled to the brim with politics ', as had been said of him, had not foreseen what would happen. His party had never abandoned the old colours, nor the idea of a ' people's Empire ' which by a decision of the democracy would take the place of the Republic. The idea was less in favour, less talked of ; it had no longer the aspect of a national hope as in the days of distress after the defeat. But the halls for the party meetings were still decorated with the black, white, and red, even when the German Foreign Minister was the speaker. It was a romantic *naïveté* on the part of people to believe this consistent. There was both romance and *naïveté* in Stresemann's assent to the cabinet's decision. When he had tried to end the Kapp ' putsch ' by compromise he did so because he had no feeling for the legitimacy of the Republic. Now as representative of the Republic he concluded its treaties, he had given all his strength and energy to its salvation, he would have felt very differently nowadays if an impudent attack were made on it. In the flag question he still did not feel quite in unison with it. It is not the coolness of reasoned argument, not the razor-like sharpness of critical judgement that makes a politician.

The Chancellor, who was mainly responsible, was swept away. As no one had any particular desire for a prolonged crisis, the cabinet stayed in office and the Minister of Justice, Marx, became its head. Political decisions do not strictly reflect the spirit of justice; otherwise Stresemann could not have stayed in the cabinet. It was believed that all would go well even if Luther, the able financial expert, were not there to help. But there was no question of things going well without Stresemann, who had begun the work of reconciliation, on whom it rested, who was more to the Reichstag than any party leader.

Stresemann regretted Luther's fall, but he experienced a sense of relief all the same. He had made him Finance Minister, then Chancellor. But that energetic man would not let him alone; he spoke before him and he spoke after him; he hindered more than he helped. If that was not actually the case, Stresemann's desire for independence made it appear so to him. Later on it was asked whether he himself had not brought on the crisis in order to free himself from this rather burdensome supervision. That implies a radical misapprehension. Stresemann was no Machiavellian intriguer; he was far too straight in his dealings ever to have conceived so complicated and dangerous a scheme. In any case, the motives which influenced his action are plain. It is indubitable; in the seaport towns no one knew what was the German flag. The ships flew one flag, the missions the other. That Stresemann did not see the danger which threatened the Government, himself, and, what was more important than either, his policy if the orders put Germany's attitude once again in a doubtful light—well, we know that blindness of his when sentiment overflowed. We know what happened in 1917 and 1918.

If Stresemann parted company with the Chancellor without regret, the explanation lies in a personal quality of his. Together he and Luther had gone a long part of the way, a very difficult part, and their immediate collaborators testify that they had worked together in harmony. But Stresemann was sensitive; he was becoming steadily more so. A man who had had to face and ward off so many attacks, to suffer so many reverses, must, one is often inclined to think, develop in time a really thick skin, if indeed he did not possess one originally. On the contrary, Stresemann was more thin-skinned than ever, more easily hurt. There were not a few men in political life whom he could not endure for long without a real effort, a severe exercise of self-control. These were either political opponents or political friends, but were always men who had constantly or intermittently worked intimately with him. It is well known that is what happened in the case of Erzberger and Helfferich, then Schiffer and Friedberg, then Heinze, then Count Brockdorff-Rantzau whose great qualities he none the less held in high esteem, Gessler, Wirth. To the end it was so in his own party and in his own department.

His aversion cannot in the least have all been justified, but it was the result of his temperament, which was neither easy nor equable, nor robust, nor impervious to hurt, as so many thought. The spirit of a *petit bourgeois* was the basic spirit of the man. Nervous sensibility and sensitiveness had helped to take him out of and above the sphere in which he was born and bred. We spoke of the flair, which almost invariably characterized him and made him often able to foretell political consequences, to size up situations with a lightning glance. To assume lack of nerve in his relations to people brought into close contact with him would be absurd in the case of a man who possessed so brilliant a gift as flair. What he valued in men, what attracted him and bound him to them, was solidity, reliability, singleness of mind. Chameleon-like personalities were always unsympathetic to him who himself had been suspected by his world of changeableness and vacillation. In the heat of the political struggle of 1918 he said of Ebert: 'He does not grow with the growth of his aims.' Later, when he got to know the first President of the Republic better, he stayed true to him. Similar was his feeling towards Hindenburg, the second President. Similarly he had stayed loyal to Bassermann, and the same loyalty which he gave to leaders he showed to devoted assistants.

We have already spoken of the changes in his own career. When necessity and the recognition of it had become a component part of his thought he remained consistent. A change which is intimately connected with Luther's fall we shall later experience with him. In foreign policy he remained consistent as long as he directed it. In the autumn of 1926 he went again to Geneva. On September 8th Germany's entrance into the League was unanimously accepted. On the 9th the German delegation entered the Assembly. On the 10th there was the gala session in which 'the threateningly empty seats' were occupied for the first time. The League had to bring a victim. Spain, whose wishes in the matter of a Council seat had not been gratified, announced her withdrawal. On September 16th Stresemann for the first time represented Germany in the League Council. He should have been its President, but he asked Benès, the Czechoslovak Foreign Minister, to preside in his stead.

On September 17th there took place that renowned luncheon in the little town of Thoiry, at which Briand and Stresemann, accompanied only by a confidential interpreter, Professor Hesnard of the French Embassy in Berlin, held converse about Europe.

The intimate talk had had a preliminary history. After the unfortunate eleven days which the Germans wasted before the gates of the League, Briand and Stresemann had arranged a meeting which was to take place somewhere in France. Every time the day for it approached something occurred to prevent it. The French Government was in danger and Briand could not leave Paris. At last a meeting was fixed for July 15th. Then Herriot overthrew the Government. Stresemann, who was in Wildungen for his kidney trouble, nearly had a nervous breakdown from sheer rage.

The result was that he regarded this political excursion with the greatest nervous excitement. On the day before, when he was discussing things with journalists of Right sympathies, and, as was their wont, they indicated their objections to his policy, he burst out: 'To-morrow night you will think differently about your criticism; the facts will compel you to admit the injustice of it.' Then no one knew anything about Thoiry. Next day the two Ministers spent five hours together. In the evening a short *communiqué* was issued whose text had been agreed upon. In this it was said that they had brought 'their conceptions into harmony'. Briand spoke to interviewers about an 'atmosphere of confidence'; Stresemann of the 'Franco-German understanding as the corner-stone of the European understanding' and of proposals 'not on details but for a general solution'. While the whole world, filled with the deepest interest, waited for more information, not another word was said for three days.

September 21st was a strenuous day. For many hours Stresemann negotiated on technical matters with Sir Eric Drummond, the Secretary-General of the League of Nations. At midday he met the representatives of Danzig and Memel. He attended a farewell dinner in the evening to the parliamentary members of the German delegation, which was marked by great cordiality. After midnight only he got down to the banquet of the German Associations in Geneva in the Gambrinus Hall. The gathering had been waiting for him since nine o'clock. The guest of honour delivered a great speech, one of those compelling speeches of his whereby he could sway his hearers—even those who disagreed with him—as he wished. The enthusiasm was boundless.

There has been so much discussion over this 'Gambrinus speech', it aroused feeling in more countries than one. First of all reports appeared from the agencies, then an official text appeared, according to which much had apparently not been said which many believed they had heard being said. A wave of romantic feeling had swept over Stresemann. He saw his beloved Fatherland far farther on than it actually was. The occupation troops gone from the Rhineland, the Saar basin restored to the Republic, colonial mandates handed out to Germany, and, as all appeared so beautiful, the opposition of the Nationalists was incomprehensible, those cavillers for whom nothing went fast enough, and who were no longer capable of trust in a leader.

That was not the last time, as it was not the first time, that the romantic vision of Stresemann had seen things near at hand which were far off. The actual result of the conversations at Thoiry was a scheme for mobilizing the State railways' bonds and handing over to France at once a large payment in gold. For that evacuation would be accelerated. It turned out that there was no market for the bonds.

'From illusions to disillusionments,' Count Westarp had said, 'from disillusionments to new illusions.' Did he judge rightly? Only the man who quickly recovered from disillusionment, whom inexhaustible stores of hope made able to mount a new attack immediately after a repulse could travel the road that led from the Ruhr war to the restoration of the currency and the budget, from revolution and counter-revolution to work in assured peace, from separatism to secured unity, from the eleven days of waiting to Thoiry, from the Gambrinus Hall to the Hague.

Germany's entry into the League was, too, but a beginning. There remained questions enough, every one of great importance, every one well able to create difficulties, every one concealing danger to the relations of the Locarno Powers. The Inter-Allied Commission of Control was still in Germany, an insult to German self-esteem. And when it was dissolved on January 31, 1927, there remained the problem of the right of investigation and search, whether disarmed Germany was or was not arming again. There remained the question of the reduction of the armies of occupation, so long as complete evacuation was not obtained. There remained the question of disarmament. Germany had disarmed. But not one of the victor States had begun to disarm. Some believed that things were progressing; others that they were progressing very, very slowly.

The world honoured Stresemann. The Nobel Committee decided on December 9, 1926, to award him, together with Briand, Chamberlain, and Dawes, the Nobel Peace Prize.

CHAPTER IX

THE LEADER OF THE NATION

AFTER a crisis which had lasted forty-six days the Nationalists entered the cabinet, but there was no change in foreign policy. The elections of May 20, 1928, brought further losses to the People's Party and the Democrats; the Socialists and the Communists won seats. The Nationalists lost a quarter of their seats and again went into opposition. The Government of the Republic passed to a cabinet based on a 'Grand Coalition', but once again foreign policy remained unchanged. There were many disputed points in that policy, but the course which Stresemann kept was simple and straight. Versatile, nimble-minded though he was, he never swerved from it.

He was the chief speaker at a Bismarck celebration of the East Prussian regimental associations. 'The statesman who won the greatest successes in the field of foreign policy was so sceptical about the possibility of forecasting what would happen in the near future that he refused even to prophesy that either this or that would happen within the course of the next few hours. "Policy," he said, "is an occupation which is only comparable to sailing an unknown sea. There is no way of knowing what weather, what currents, what gales one will encounter. And in politics there is the additional disadvantage that one has to depend upon and

STRESEMANN AND THE LEAGUE OF NATIONS

A PHOTOGRAPH TAKEN AT LUGANO IN DECEMBER 1928

Herr Stresemann conversing with M. Procopé, the Finnish Foreign Minister

reckon with the decisions of others, that it is never possible to negotiate in perfect freedom, and if the allies on whose support one counted change their minds for apparently no particular reason at all, then one's whole policy suffers shipwreck ".'

Was he thinking of Thoiry? Or that the colonial mandates, announced just after Locarno, had not yet been handed to Germany? A cash payment was to secure that Eupen and Malmédy be allowed to decide themselves whether or no they desired to return to Germany. But nothing is happening. The Rhineland is still occupied. The evacuation, it is true, is proceeding, but it is proceeding very slowly—too slowly for one who is a romantic where the future of the Fatherland is concerned. Often he lies sleepless and dreams dreams. The Eiffel Tower will crash to the ground and the French General Staff at such a sign and a wonder will turn Christian. A new continent will rise out of the ocean and Poland will hand back the corridor. There is a child in every man, a child who wants to play—with unknown possibilities, with the help of Heaven.

Yet no one can be so sure of his policy, that 'incalculable' policy, so sure of himself. There is a tavern in Geneva town called 'Bavaria', where in an atmosphere thick with smoke, journalists and folk on the fringe of diplomacy are wont to sit, Germans of differing political views, Frenchmen, Czechs. Down comes the Foreign Minister of Germany from a dinner at his English colleagues' with the Secretary of State. 'Good evening, gentlemen.' He sits down and within a minute discussion is in full swing.

Briand, the old Socialist, goes home at night ; as he says himself, he ' is not up to the excesses of Calvinist conviviality '. The exponent of the oldest diplomacy, Austen Chamberlain, travels from London to Dover in the same train as the journalists, from Dover to Calais in the same ship, from Calais to Paris, from Paris to Geneva in the same train. None of them succeed in speaking to him. On his way to the dining-car he has to pass the journalists' compartments ; he keeps his head down, his eyes staring straight in front so that he need not greet them. Stresemann argues in the hotel lounge with a journalist of the Left. In Berlin he boycotts restaurants which do not exhibit the black, red, and gold flag. The Minister does not like that. The clear voice is emphatic : ' You are no friends of the Republic.' His audience sits round him, and any one who happens to be near joins the crowd. In ' Bavaria ' the journalists listen to the talk. A Social Democrat questions him. Why did he in 1923 force his party to leave the Government ? Would he do the same next time ? Stresemann argues : ' That is not so. The responsible party was the party itself.' He himself is prepared to co-operate with whoever will co-operate with him. The journalist protests angrily, but he cannot talk the Minister down. Strangers become interested. Their countries are not perhaps quite so democratic ; they receive a lesson in democracy.

The high officials in the diplomatic service do not quite approve. The representative of a great State —is it right that among foreigners he should defend his policy in a public-house ? Is that quite correct ? A day or two later the delegations hear from the foreign journalists what the dispute was about. Ministers of States great and small cannot hide a slight feeling of envy. Happy the statesman who can face public opinion so confidently.

Stresemann would scarcely agree with the officials that he suffered loss of dignity. After his work is done, and after the formal circumstances under which the work is done, off he goes to his usual table to drink a glass of beer. He is a student again, a bourgeois, neither aesthete nor snob. In honour of his friend Bassermann, an old corps student, he once wrote: 'This Germany of ours for which we strive is not represented by the aesthetes in the cafés of the capital. Nay, it is in the villages where our German parsons bide, in our peasant holdings and country mansions, in the little provincial towns, aye, at that so often derided regular table of ours in the beer-parlours, among our honest German middle class, in town and country where folk are not so highly educated as not to be able to enjoy German songs and German singing, German stories and German wit, where folk think more of the East Sea and the North Sea, of the Hartz and the Giant Mountains than of Monte Carlo and St. Moritz—there what is deepest in us has its deepest roots.'

Prince Bernhard von Bülow, that precise observer of political events and political currents, who weighs his words and needed in his old age to desire the favour of none, wrote in reply to a request for his opinion of Stresemann: 'He is the most notable figure of the new parliamentary Germany, and as Foreign Minister has shown qualities which have extorted the respect of the foreigner. His conception of the national dignity is clear and simple. It is rooted in his own character. Each of his opponents in negotiations has to reckon with it as an important factor. In Geneva he won sympathies which are not to be lightly esteemed.' How different the age, how different the methods, when Bülow was the political guide of the Empire!

Another who approached him from a very different side, but who saw no less clearly, Maximilian Harden, answered Bülow when he called Stresemann 'the best Foreign Minister of the latest age' with the malicious question: 'Do you reckon the latest age from Bethmann or from Bülow?'

. . . . .

Clear, common, prosy sense won the victory over romantic ardour. Yet Stresemann permitted himself one last return to it. In 1927 he had to deliver the oration at the sixtieth anniversary of the National Liberal, now the German People's Party. Eight years before he had spoken of a Sabbath hour which had been devoted only to the recollection of the past, and the party conference had applauded him. Six years ago he had temporized; he had said that, if the party made alliance with the Left, 'intellect and feeling were in conflict'. Now quietly he led the way to the new policy with a will to win. He called himself 'a wanderer between two political worlds'. He spoke 'of the old Germany which we loved and the new Germany for which we live'. 'We will not refuse to hearken to the call to work with and for our country, the German Republic. And we shall accept unpopularity rather than pursue an easy policy of agitation.' He named Bismarck, and immediately afterwards 'the men of the Paulskirche', and then 'the black, red, and gold sash of the German students'. The hall in which the conference was held was decorated with black, white, and red flags.

Not that he had rooted out his romantic love of Germany's past. His conception of it had changed. It went further back; it became critical; it could distinguish between 'the simplicity and the dignity of the great age of Wilhelm I' and 'the age of pomp, of outward show, of satiety'. It had become necessary to pass from the old flag to the new. But the new flag was still the old one. And when one considered the age of the Imperial flag things were not quite so good as they seemed after the Revolution. Stresemann's judgement was acute if sentiment did not lead it astray.

'After the foundation of the Empire we fell into a period of crass materialism. Just as the endless tenements of the growing cities of Germany marked the decline in architectural art, so men's whole conception of life became purely materialist. The decline in literature, the frivolity of the drama, the substitution of music-hall ditties for the old folk-songs, these were phenomena contemporary with a prodigious economic and technical development which made men richer in worldly wealth but poorer in happiness than ever they had been before. This was the age when there appeared that economic snobbery which considered itself above the duty of sharing in the spiritual life of the nation. There was no need to know literature old and new as long as one knew all about hundredweights and tons, about cotton, about iron goods and steel tubes, or, as to-day, about stocks and exchanges. The homes of the leaders of our economic life should have been witness to the state of German architecture and German painting, but they only began to shrug their shoulders if they found any one really concerned with such things. The joy of work of the German nation degenerated into a material lust of work which began to do away with the hours of spiritual recuperation.'

Soon after the party's sixtieth anniversary, Stresemann addressed the students of Tübingen. They were Nationalists, Fascists, without any confidence in the Foreign Minister of the Republic, the man of the League of Nations. Stresemann liked a public platform better than the Reichstag, 'the most wearisome talking-shop in the world', or the conferences of the party, 'which confines one's ideas'. Best of all he liked to speak to opponents who had to be convinced. How easy it would have been for him to have brought these young men to their feet yelling and stamping applause! All he had to do was to utter the words, 'The peace of shame' or 'The dictate of Versailles'. But he made his task difficult and yet succeeded. He went back to Stein and Scharnhorst, to the revolutionaries who saved Prussia, to the men of the Paulskirche, in order to explain to these youths what sort of man Ebert was. He had voted against the peace treaty, but now he said: 'There was a day in Weimar when to say "Aye" showed as much sense of responsibility as to say "No".' The young men with the coloured caps all thought of themselves as 'anti-Marxists'. The Minister said to them: 'No one has the right to think himself infallible. Let us learn to guide ourselves by the counsel: "Do reverence to every honest conviction before you attack it".' He knew that the students were full of the idea that they were born to lead. He said to them: 'You stand amid the people.' Stresemann was always a gifted speaker. But now there was a difference. Now he spoke against his audience in order to win it. When he left he had won a German University for the Republic without ever having uttered the word.

Next year he went a step further. Addressing the 'Union of German Students', which was an organization of the Right, he adopted a phrase used by his party associate, the eighty-year-old Professor Kahl, who had declared that it was necessary 'to defend the Republic with one's life'. In the same year he spoke at Minden to the National Conference of German Youth of the People's Party. The young party members should go on the quest for the black, red, and gold flag. For one day the Minister came amongst them. All over the hall waved black, white, and red flags. Had he played the traitor? Was this latest development treachery? The explanation was so simple. He had saved the Republic at the hour of its greatest need. When it slowly emerged from its difficulties, he had led it. It had become his republic. Now, therefore, he stood under the black, red, and gold colours.

The Minister had time. He conducted the foreign policy of the Republic, he led Parliament, he led his party. It was extraordinary how much time he had. In Berlin there was produced the *Neidhard von Gneisenau* of a gifted young playwright. In it Blücher in comparison with the uncomprehended genius of the hero was only an idiot. The parallel was clear and the public was clever enough to seize upon it loudly or quietly. Stresemann, when he went on leave to San Remo, took a case full of books with him to refute the false thesis. He wrote a comprehensive article, in which he defended the brave national hero. And since the desire to write history took him, he turned also to the defence of the king, whom the dramatist had made even sillier and placed in a still more ungrateful position. He was much prouder of this work than of his biggest Reichstag speeches and let every one see it—journalists, diplomatists, and even the nuncio.

He found time to speak on ‘ Goethe and the War of Independence ’, to defend the dazzled poet against the charge of lacking national sentiment. He had time to deliver an address before actors of all nations in the Stage Club against the over-estimation of sport, against the technicalization of the age, against jazz, which he could not abide, expressing his scepticism on wireless and the cinema, and defending the spoken word directly heard by the audience as the sole medium through which the depths of the spirit could be revealed.

He would have had still more time if he had not turned ill. Even in these last days at Geneva, when the referendum of the Right which equated his policy to high treason, rose up threateningly against him he groaned : ‘ If I could I would visit every university and *I* would win the students.’ He was a true student himself. Even when he was a Minister he loved to wear the scarf and the cap. Berlin and Leipzig, where he studied, are great cosmopolitan cities in which the university is in the background.

Heidelberg, which conferred an honorary degree upon him, became his academic home by preference. There he sat in the last year of his life, in a students' café, drinking the beer, which the doctors had forbidden, with his friends, with young university men and attachés. When he was in Berlin and went into Hessler's café, a thing he was very fond of doing, the band used to play, 'I Lost My Heart in Heidelberg'. 'In my honour,' said the Minister, not without pride. He remained a student all his life. It pained him when the young men of the universities did not understand his policy.

The German People's Party, which had entered the National Assembly only twenty-two strong, had sixty-five members in the first Reichstag. After the election of 1924 it was fifty-one strong, in 1928 forty-five. The heavy industries whose election contributions were so necessary turned towards the Nationalists. There is no doubt that under Stresemann's leadership the party declined. There were many reasons for that, sociological, and not merely political, ones. But there certainly were political ones. The Democrats had preceded the People's Party in defeat. In the National Assembly they had numbered seventy-five; in 1928 they were reduced to twenty-five. The policy of conciliation brought victory to the Social Democrats—they had one hundred and fifty-two seats—but not to the middle-class parties. It was certainly a great honour for the party that the man who for years controlled the foreign policy of the Republic was one of its members. But to the good party man that was a cause of anxiety as well as pride.

It was said that Stresemann was of capital

importance for the world and for Europe, for Germany and for the Reichstag; he had no place in his own party. That could be true at a moment when leader and party were out of humour with each other, and at such moments it certainly was true. But he always brought the party, within Parliament and without, over to his view again, and it always let itself be brought over, in spite of the sacrifice in popularity which was paid in loss of votes. Without the support of the Parliamentary party he would not have remained its representative in the Government. He was a Parliamentarian, and he knew precisely what the value of respective strengths was; he had no wish to be a general without troops or to have no basis either for his ministerial position or his policy. The party went to the election of 1928 with his portrait on their placards and the motto:

> Let others go what way they can,
> You vote with Gustav Stresemann.

Although he was already a sick man he went into the lions' den to speak for the party: he went to Munich. In the Bürgerbrau, where he was to speak, women waved strips of silver stuff—'the silver lining in the clouds'; Fascists and Nationalists under Hitler's leadership yelled him down; the members of the Stahlhelm, for whom he had so often expressed his sympathy, did not trouble to defend him.

At the conferences of the party organizations the black, red, and gold flags became ever more prominent. He himself at the National Conference of its young members at Minden had turned the tide in their favour. He no longer understood the point of view which had so lately been his own. He was intransigeant. 'How *can* the German Nationalists . . . ?' he said angrily. To a woman member of the party, who defended the maintenance of the black, white, and red flag, he said: 'What, you too? I cannot understand you.' It had come to that, that he no longer understood. The position was clear, the transformation necessary. The weight of sentiment had broken all barriers down.

To the day of his death the party, though often only with great reluctance, went with him. When he was buried the wreath of the German People's Party was adorned with black, white, and red ribbons.

It was at Christmas of 1927 that Stresemann's health began to be seriously affected. In May 1928 the world was shocked to read an official medical bulletin. All the celebrations for his fiftieth birthday were cancelled. The Minister had wanted just at that time to speak again in Munich. It was impossible. For long he had not been well enough. That very German way of life of his, full of restless activity and spiritual excitement, with his student's love of seeking recreation over wine or beer, had asked too much of a nervous and delicate constitution. He looked, but was anything but, robust. His kidneys were seriously affected; his heart could not answer the demand made on it. It beat too quickly in its effort to drive the blood through the veins. Since his breakdown in May it was known that the days of the Minister were numbered. The finger of death had touched him. A doctor must always be in the neighbourhood, a nurse be in attendance. His diet was strictly regulated; wine and beer must be given up. Had he resigned his post and gone to Egypt, where the dry climate is so good for kidney troubles, he might have made the span allotted to him extend over years.

He had personal reasons, too, for resigning. He was not a man of property. He had had the income of a rich man before he became minister. But his capital, his savings, had been seriously decreased at the inflation period. The Republic did not pay its highest political servants very generously. He did not wish to appear stingy while abroad on his country's service. Many knew that his generosity was the worst foe of his bank balance. The Nobel Prize—he shared it with Briand—vanished as quickly as a drop of water on a hot stone. Once he went out of office the most lucrative posts, any directorship he liked, were there for him. Articles for the Press, books of memoirs would bring in huge sums. His wife, his two young sons, the one a ministerial official, the other a student, might well have enforced their claims on husband and father. Other great officials had made no bones about giving up the service of the State when there were great prizes to be won outside it. Stresemann stayed at his post.

The cabinet crisis after the elections did not last any less long than was usual. On May 20th the nation had given a decision which could only be interpreted as a demand for a Grand Coalition. The parliamentary parties could not agree; the gulf between the Social Democrats and the People's Party seemed unbridgeable. On June 22nd the new Chancellor, the Social Democrat Hermann Müller, asked Stresemann whether without the support of his party he would enter a Weimar

Coalition cabinet as an expert, or would enter a 'cabinet of notables'. Stresemann was lying ill in a sanatorium at Bühl in Baden. He answered in the negative. Co-operation between the Social Democrats and the People's Party was possible and necessary. He demanded, in conformity to the spirit of the Constitution, the formation of a ministry apart altogether from party resolutions, and promised his own co-operation and that of his friend Curtius.

His communication was known as 'the bolt from Bühl'. It cleared up the foggy atmosphere in Parliament. The construction of the cabinet made progress. On June 28th the President of the Republic was able to sign the decrees of appointment.

Stresemann had wounded his party comrades. The telegram to Hermann Müller was at the same time sent to the leader of the Parliamentary Party, but as he was not in his office during the week-end it only reached him later. The result was a good deal of ill-humour. The misunderstanding went so far that in the official Party organ, the *Nationalliberalen Korrespondenz*, closer contact between leader and Party was demanded. The Parliamentary Party believed that a march had been stolen upon it. A resolution showed full confidence in the parliamentary leader, but was a demonstration against the party's head. When the cabinet was finally completed the Parliamentary Party declared that it was in no way bound to the Government. A fundamental difference of opinion which concerned the fundamental problem of the German democracy seemed unavoidable. Should the parties follow their leaders, should all decisions of the leaders be the result of a majority vote in the parties? This time the conflict was postponed although a satisfactory ending to it would have been a great gain to Germany. Stresemann was not allowed to fight the issue through.

Stresemann went for a cure to Karlsbad, and then to Oberhof in Thuringia. Here death again knocked at the door. A blood-vessel burst in the brain. Speech had ever come at his command; speech had liberated, had exalted him. Now that faculty was gone. Even after he returned to Berlin ordinary words failed him; he sought for them painfully and could not find them. In a couple of days this dangerous symptom disappeared. Again he was in full control of his best instrument.

On August 27th the signature took place in Paris of the Kellogg Pact, whereby the United States, France, Belgium, Czechoslovakia, Britain, Germany, Japan, and Poland formally declared: 'We renounce war as a method of solution of international difficulties. We renounce this instrument of national policy.' Stresemann, friendlily received by the population of the French capital, signed the Pact for Germany. He had a conversation with the President of the Council, Poincaré. Such a meeting was full of symbolic significance. After more than an hour had passed, Stresemann's doctor, who trembled for his patient, sent a card into the conference-room. The card by mistake was taken to Poincaré. On it was written: 'You have talked enough; let us see deeds now.' Only later was it possible to let the astonished President know that the warning was not meant for him.

When the League of Nations met, the Minister for Foreign Affairs was not allowed to travel. The doctors forbade him. In his stead the Chancellor went to Geneva. Asked to discuss Germany's most serious problem by a representative of an international Press service he said: 'The whole German nation expects to see the Rhineland freed from the armies of occupation.' He did not succeed in getting a date for that fixed.

At the end of November, Stresemann spoke in the Reichstag: 'Germany's rights are injured so long as her claim to the evacuation of the Rhineland is not given effect to.' The leader of the Nationalists, Count Westarp, flung the taunt at him: 'The episode of the so-called Locarno policy is over. France threatens Germany's security. Her troops remain on the Rhine, and on German soil she holds, with the British, manœuvres on an unprecedented scale.' That was true; the commanders of the armies of occupation had amused themselves with the holding of manœuvres in the Rhineland. Strategic idea: attack eastwards.

In December the Council of the League of Nations met at Lugano, only an hour's journey away from Locarno, from the blue waters of reconciliation. Once again Briand, Chamberlain, Stresemann met. Three years had passed since Europe had been placed on a new basis. And the generals of the Western States were indulging their passion for activity by holding manœuvres in the Rhineland. Stresemann put direct questions to France and Britain, which showed his impatience. It was agreed that experts should again meet and examine Germany's capacity to pay and the reparations problem.

At the last session of the Council the Polish Foreign Minister, Zaleski, reported on the question of the German minority in Upper Silesia. Everything would go on perfectly if the German People's League would stop making difficulties, would stop making complaints. Even while Zaleski was speaking, Stresemann had struck the table with his fist. He leaped to his feet the moment the Pole had finished. 'This is a scandal. You say we are just wasting time here.' If the League of Nations did not protect the rights of minorities then the whole basis on which it stood was destroyed. In history it is often the reverse of helpful to strike the green table with one's fist. But the action can also bring solutions, bring liberation. It is an affair of feeling, of flair, if the outburst of an oppressed heart, of strained nerves, can improve the situation.

In the spring of 1929 the economic experts met in Paris, under the chairmanship of the American, Young, to advise on a new plan for German reparations. While the eyes of every German with any political sense at all were focused anxiously on Paris, there was a political crisis in Berlin. It was a double crisis, for both the national and the Prussian Governments were involved. The parliamentary parties thought themselves hurt because their influence was not strong enough in the cabinet in proportion to their numbers, deputies thought that they ought finally to press their irrefragable claims to seats in the cabinet. The Centrists came out of the national Government in the sulks ; the People's Party wanted to enter the Prussian Government. It was a war of all against all which had broken out among the legislators, and the nation watched it without being able to understand the reasons for it.

Stresemann summoned the central committee of

THE GERMANS IN PARIS

A PHOTOGRAPH TAKEN ON THE BALCONY OF THE QUAI D'ORSAY

Left to right: Herr Stresemann, State Secretary von Schubert, and Herr von Hoesch, German Ambassador in Paris

the People's Party, a body of several hundred members. Many who had grounds for dissatisfaction thought that the claims of both sections would now be discussed to the roots. Cards were seen in many hands on which were written down questions prepared with endless trouble and precision. The party leader spoke seven sentences in which he outlined the parliamentary situation. He spoke for two hours on the parliamentary crisis, on the caricature which the parliamentary system in Germany had become, on the completely false conception of Parliament which now obtained, on his own responsibility to the nation. On the folly of the parliamentary parties wanting to elect, appoint, and withdraw ministers. On the insult to the President of the Republic which the presumption of the parties implied. On the fatal rivalry of the parties in their mad race for popularity. On the grotesque picture of the Government parties forming the opposition to the Government. Finally that the spirit of party must recognize its just limits.

It was a great speech, the last which Stresemann delivered on home politics, a speech which it would be good for parliamentarians to hear every year until it had some effect. It can be understood that not all his hearers were pleased. But throughout the country it won the applause of every patriot.

The Paris conference was one of agitations and commotions. The sick Minister followed feverishly its troubles from Germany while the doctors sought to maintain his strength. The director of the Reichsbank, Schacht, made a powerful inroad into the domain of politics. The conference was on the verge of collapse when the British delegate, Lord

Revelstoke, died. His death saved it. The German expert, Vogler, the representative of the heavy industries, left the German delegation. Unable to help, Stresemann watched from a distance; every crisis fell like a blow on his tortured body. 'They are destroying my hopes of evacuation, of the liberation of the Rhineland.' He felt, if he did not actually know, that he would not long be spared to work for his country. Others might have time to indulge in side-issues, in diversions, in tactical manœuvres. He had not. It was a race between death the incalculable and international politics. Which would reach the goal first?

But the conference of experts did finally end, and with a positive result. In summer there came the political conference in the Hague which should give political effect to the Young Plan. Poincaré, a stricken man, had retired. Briand, now President of the Council as well as Foreign Minister, was the more hampered in his actions. In England the Conservatives had been defeated at the elections. The Labour Government, a minority Government, had every reason to seek to strengthen their position at home by a brilliant success abroad. Snowden, the British Chancellor of the Exchequer, was a firebrand, and, as if made hard in the fire, with a reckless disregard of consequences, began a bitter fight with every other nation. He demanded an increase in the British share of the reparations and sought to show, if necessary violently, that there was to be no more of Chamberlain's complacency to France.

The German delegation, Stresemann and three of his colleagues, sat waiting. Since Locarno he had conducted his policy with the Western States united. Every time Britain and France had been at variance Germany had paid the costs of the quarrel. One ill-considered move and the same fatal event would occur again. Stresemann, not robust by nature, sensitive, easily wounded, had never been able to endure stoically if politics went against him, against Germany. Now his sensitiveness was increased, was at its height; he was immeasurably disturbed—and he determined to remain unperturbed.

He asked Briand when France would evacuate the Rhineland. Briand answered that the commanders had informed him that it was impossible to move the troops in the winter. Extraordinary, commented Stresemann, it was in the depth of winter that troops were moved into the Ruhr. His colleagues were angry; he asked them to consider: 'Suppose a victorious Ludendorff had been the commander-in-chief in Germany. Things would not have been very easy for a German Minister for Foreign Affairs.'

To a Press conference he complained: 'The Treasury wants to ruin German industry.' When he was contradicted, there was a fresh outburst. Then he forced himself to admit that there was no positive proof that such a calamity threatened.

But Briand's refusal for weeks to come to any decision on important points made it difficult to keep silence, perhaps meant bitter disappointment to Stresemann. The scheme for control of the Rhineland disguised under the innocuous name of a 'Commission of Information and Conciliation' was a recognized matter for negotiation since the Geneva session at which the sick Minister had been unable to be present. Such a commission would only serve to envenom the relations between the Rhine States. But it was a scheme dear to the military, whose aim was always security rather than conciliation. It cost a mighty effort to get rid of this fatal scheme. The whole business had to be dourly fought while the obstinate Snowden fiercely maintained his standpoint and the conference remained in danger. If it parted without reaching a decision, the Young Plan fell through and evacuation delayed no one knew how long.

But that was not the only care. In Germany there was the referendum demanded by the Nationalist leader, Hugenberg, the general onslaught on Stresemann's policy, aye, on the Republic. Stresemann's nerves were submitted to their hardest ordeal; in the privacy of intimacy they gave way. He thought himself abandoned by the Press of the Left; he suspected that he was personally opposed by a section of his own delegation. Much, too much, lay on his shoulders. He wanted to resign. A politician came hastily from Berlin to beg him to stay at his post. All persuasion seemed to be without effect. He held to his opinion—he would resign. Until the other said to him: 'Would you like, Herr X. to become Foreign Minister?' Herr X. was a deputy whose temperament Stresemann feared would not let him stay within the narrow limits of his own policy. He answered: 'I shall carry on.'

Red light shone from the Minister's eyes when he was angry. Tiny blood-vessels in them burst. Once before, at Oberhof, a small blood-vessel had burst and deprived him of the power of speech. Any day in the Hague another, a little bigger, a little more important, might do the same.

At a night meeting which lasted overlong he fell back, clutched at his heart, and said : ' It's all over.' The German Finance Minister, once a doctor, felt his pulse and found it faint, irregular, warning danger.

At last a compromise with Snowden was reached. All the nations had to consent to sacrifices so that the grim Chancellor might make peace. Chamberlain has declared his opinion that it was Stresemann's hand that saved the conference from failure. The Labour Government declared that no British soldier would remain longer on the Rhine. The ' Conciliation Commission ', which made conciliation doubtful, was no longer a subject of debate. The French commanders came to the conclusion that at a snail's pace the troops could at once be moved back fifteen kilometres. The final date for evacuation was fixed. On June 30, 1930, German soil would be finally liberated.

. . . . .

Let us pause here a moment. Something great had happened.

The Treaty of Versailles, cruel as it was for Germany, had not come up to the expectations of the French Chauvinists and military men. They believed that they could not sleep peacefully o' nights if France's frontier were not on the Rhine. Five years after the conclusion of peace their hopes seemed very near realization. Not merely did adventurers and hired ruffians call for the Rhenish Republic, but calm, sensible men, as we can remember, supported the ' policy of scuttle ', and asked in amazement: 'Do you really imagine that the French will ever get out?' Stresemann, who raised the Republic from the depths of its misery, who saw 'the silver lining in the cloud', was laughed at. Five more years had passed. The date was fixed, it was rapidly approaching, when there would not be a single foreign soldier on German soil.

There had been great changes. The man of 'the People's Empire', the man of the black, white, and red flag, who passed Sabbath hours in dreaming of the past, speaks: 'In July we shall have a black, red, and gold celebration.'

He who was as able to enjoy festivities as he was able to work hard, lay at the last celebration of all under wreaths of flowers. The black, red, and gold flag waved over his coffin.

. . . . .

From the Hague, Stresemann went to Geneva. The man who had exhausted himself clearing away the rubbish of the past now spoke of the future. In the League Assembly he asked: 'Where is the European currency; where are the postage stamps of Europe?' Every one knew what it meant if such marks of sovereignty bore the superscription 'Europe'.

'Every great ideal seems at first stupidity. I refuse to regard the economic confederation of Europe to be a Utopia.' The way that European frontiers were drawn to-day would in a few decades seem like something out of the Middle Ages.

The liberation of the Fatherland lay in Stresemann's hand. Yet it was an unarmed nation among neighbours bristling with weapons. To arm it again meant to invite another destruction. To him security was a continental idea. 'The German nation, conquered, disarmed, seeks in more than one field new ways of human progress.' So he said on the anniversary of the Constitution on August 11th. He was the man who at no moment, not even in its deepest humiliation, had ceased to treat his nation otherwise than if she were a Great Power, as her numbers and her achievements demanded. But the period of 'as if' of necessity came to an end. The man with death in his heart who for the last time spoke to the world, who loved the Germany of the future as he had loved the Germany of the past, saw her once again stand in her greatness in the new Europe.

On the way home he stopped at the Vierwaldstättersee. He now began his day a weary man. Only when political discussion warmed him did he become fresh and bright. The referendum, which was meant to insult him, equated his policy to high treason. The Nationalist Press attacked him more bitterly than ever. He was accused of selling Germany into slavery, of forcing the coming generations under a foreign yoke. He declared that he no longer read the Nationalist papers. He became steadily more sensitive, more thin-skinned. Things now seemed scarcely bearable. 'Now for the first time I know what cutting one to the quick means. I experience that sensation every time my opponents befoul me.'

At Vitznau he spoke about the founding of a great middle-class party. It should be the party of the Liberal *bourgeoisie*, the 'nationally conscious'. From the left and right of him men would join him, avow his aims. He remembered one of the sentences in the Paulskirche: 'The ease with which many of our youth despair of the future of the Fatherland is one of the most repulsive phenomena of the present age.' His great new party would include all those who like himself had joyous confidence in the future of Germany.

He arrived in Berlin when a parliamentary crisis was in full swing. On the question of unemployment insurance the conflicting interests of employers and employed seemed impossible to reconcile. He went to a party meeting, grappled with the apparently insoluble problem, carried his colleagues along with him. While he was speaking some one called out: 'You only want to remain Minister and *we* have got to pay for that.' Stresemann made the compromise which held the Government together and made it capable of making head against all the efforts of the partisans of dictatorship.

He should not have been speaking, working, rousing himself to effort. He should have been in Egypt and not in the Reichstag, not in the Wilhelmstrasse. His heart, steadily overworked as years went on, could no longer perform its functions. His cheeks were sunken, the veins stood out on his temples. In Geneva a Hungarian cartoonist had sought to draw him. Suddenly his hand fell; he had stopped. A caricature? No, here was no subject for the cartoonist's pencil.

The tiny blood-vessels in the head, choked with blood and matter, which was not swiftly enough carried away, had waited for long for something to give way.

In the evening when he went to bed one of them

swelled, burst. The brain was affected; he lost consciousness; one side of his body was paralysed; the mouth which so magnificently, so victoriously had mastered language, rattled. At half-past six in the morning of October, 1929, death, which had so long been at work, ended its task.

The world honoured the dead as it had honoured no other German of the new epoch. A great statesman, a great European, a great patriot, they said, was dead.

The President of the Republic, General Field-Marshal von Hindenburg, now fourscore years and two, walked behind the coffin.

. . . . .

The figure of Stresemann remains a subject of controversy. Admired and loved, reviled and hated.

It may be as you will, but in these years, at a turning-point in history, he was Germany.

SOURCES

FOR Stresemann's early life, the reminiscences published by GEORG SCHWIDETZKY in the *Koelnische Zeitung* have been of the greatest service. I took the *curriculum vitae* from ROCHUS, FREIHERR VON RHEINBABEN'S book *Stresemann, the Man and the Statesman* (English translation, London, 1929). Details on Stresemann's activities in Saxony I found in FRANZ MIETHKE'S little work *Dr. Gustav Stresemann, der Wirtschaftspolitiker* (Sächsische Verlagsanstalt). A remarkably clear survey of the history of the war and post-war period I found in ARTUR ROSENBERG'S *Die Entstehung der Deutschen Republic* (Rowōlht) ; of the history of reparations, CARL BERGMANN'S *History of Reparations* (English translation, Benn, 1927), of the history of the conferences WOLF VON DEWALL'S *Der Kampf um den Frieden* (Frankfurter Societätsdruckerei) ; of the peri od in which Stresemann was Chancellor HENRY BERNHARD'S *Das Kabinett Stresemann* (Staatspolitischer Verlag).

Further, I made use of *Die Ursachen des Deutschen Zusammenbruchs* (the work of the investigation committee, published by the Deutsche Verlag für Politik und Geschichte) ; *Zehn Jahre Deutsche Geschichte 1918 bis 1928* (Otto Stohlberg Verlag) ; PRINCE MAX OF BADEN'S *Reminiscences* (English translation, Constable, 1928) ; M. ERZBERGER'S *Erlebnisse im Weltkrieg* (Deutsche Verlagsanstalt) ; CONRAD HAUSSMANN'S *Schlaglichter* (Frankfurter Societätsdruckerei) ; FRIEDRICH PAYER'S *Von Bethmann Hollweg bis Ebert* (ib.) ; PHILIPP SCHEIDEMANN'S *Der Zusammenbruch* (Verlag für Sozialwissenschaft) ; ERICH LUDENDORFF'S *My War Memories* (English translation, Hutchinson, 1920) ; A. KEMPKES' *Deutscher Aufbau* (Staatspolitischer Verlag) ; JOHANNES HOHLFELD'S *Geschichte der Deutschen Reiches*

1871–1926 (Verlag S. Hirzel) ; SCHULTHESS' *Europäischer Geschichtskalendar* ; THEODOR ESCHENBURG'S *Das Kaiserreich am Scheideweg* (Verlag für Kulturpolitik). Finally, there is rich material on the secret history of contemporary politics in VISCOUNT D'ABERNON'S *An Ambassador of Peace* (Hodder & Stoughton, 1928, 1929).

For many months I was hard at work investigating Stresemann's achievement, thinking, estimating.

When he died my task was about three-quarters finished. My intention was to explain the often misunderstood figure of the living statesman ; it is a sad blow to Germany that my study has become a memorial to the dead.

RUDOLF OLDEN

BERLIN, *November 1, 1929*

INDEX

PRINTED BY
JARROLD AND SONS LTD.
NORWICH

METHUEN'S
GENERAL LITERATURE

A SELECTION OF

MESSRS. METHUEN'S PUBLICATIONS

This Catalogue contains only a selection of the more important books published by Messrs. Methuen. A complete catalogue of their publications may be obtained on application.

ARMSTRONG (Anthony) ('A. A.' of Punch)
WARRIORS AT EASE
WARRIORS STILL AT EASE
PERCIVAL AND I
PERCIVAL AT PLAY
APPLE AND PERCIVAL
ME AND FRANCES
HOW TO DO IT
Each 3*s*. 6*d*. *net*.
LIVESTOCK IN BARRACKS
Illustrated by E. H. SHEPARD.
6*s*. *net*.
TWO LEGS AND FOUR
Illustrated by RENÉ BULL.
5*s*. *net*.

BAGENAL (Hope) and WOOD (Alex.)
PLANNING FOR GOOD ACOUSTICS
Illustrated. £1 2*s*. 6*d*. *net*.

BAIKIE (James)
EGYPTIAN ANTIQUITIES IN THE NILE VALLEY. Illustrated. £1 1*s*. *net*.

BAIN (F. W.)
A DIGIT OF THE MOON
THE DESCENT OF THE SUN
A HEIFER OF THE DAWN
IN THE GREAT GOD'S HAIR
A DRAUGHT OF THE BLUE
AN ESSENCE OF THE DUSK
AN INCARNATION OF THE SNOW
A MINE OF FAULTS
THE ASHES OF A GOD
BUBBLES OF THE FOAM
A SYRUP OF THE BEES
THE LIVERY OF EVE
THE SUBSTANCE OF A DREAM
Each 3*s*. 6*d*. *net*.
AN ECHO OF THE SPHERES
10*s*. 6*d*. *net*.

BALFOUR (Sir Graham)
THE LIFE OF ROBERT LOUIS STEVENSON
Twenty-first Edition. 10*s*. 6*d*. *net*.

BARKER (Ernest)
NATIONAL CHARACTER
10*s*. 6*d*. *net*.
GREEK POLITICAL THEORY
14*s*. *net*.
CHURCH, STATE AND STUDY
10*s*. 6*d*. *net*.

BELLOC (Hilaire)
PARIS 8*s*. 6*d*. *net*.
THE PYRENEES 8*s*. 6*d*. *net*.
MARIE ANTOINETTE 18*s*. *net*.
A HISTORY OF ENGLAND
In 5 Vols. Vols. I, II, III and IV
Each 15*s*. *net*.
ON NOTHING
HILLS AND THE SEA
ON SOMETHING
THIS AND THAT AND THE OTHER
ON
FIRST AND LAST
ON EVERYTHING
ON ANYTHING
EMMANUEL BURDEN
A PICKED COMPANY
Each 3*s*. 6*d*. *net*.

BIRMINGHAM (George A.)
A WAYFARER IN HUNGARY
Illustrated. 8*s.* 6*d. net.*
SPILLIKINS : ESSAYS 3*s.* 6*d. net.*
SHIPS AND SEALING-WAX : ESSAYS
3*s.* 6*d. net.*

BUDGE (Sir E. A. Wallis)
A HISTORY OF ETHIOPIA: NUBIA AND ABYSSINIA
Illustrated. 2 vols. £3 13*s.* 6*d. net.*

CHESTERTON (G. K.)
COME TO THINK OF IT . . .
6*s. net.*
G.K.C. AS M.C. 7*s.* 6*d. net.*
THE BALLAD OF THE WHITE HORSE
3*s.* 6*d. net.*
Also Illustrated by ROBERT AUSTIN. 12*s.* 6*d. net.*
CHARLES DICKENS
GENERALLY SPEAKING
ALL THINGS CONSIDERED
TREMENDOUS TRIFLES
FANCIES VERSUS FADS
ALARMS AND DISCURSIONS
A MISCELLANY OF MEN
THE USES OF DIVERSITY
THE OUTLINE OF SANITY
THE FLYING INN
Each 3*s.* 6*d. net.*
A GLEAMING COHORT 2*s.* 6*d. net.*
WINE, WATER AND SONG
1*s.* 6*d. net.*

CLUTTON-BROCK (A.)
WHAT IS THE KINGDOM OF HEAVEN ?
ESSAYS ON ART
SHAKESPEARE'S HAMLET
Each 5*s. net.*
MORE ESSAYS ON BOOKS
ESSAYS ON RELIGION
MORE ESSAYS ON RELIGION
Each 6*s. net.*
SHELLEY, THE MAN AND THE POET
Illustrated. 7*s.* 6*d. net.*
ESSAYS ON BOOKS
ESSAYS ON LITERATURE AND LIFE
ESSAYS ON LIFE *Each* 3*s.* 6*d. net.*

CRAWLEY (Ernest)
THE MYSTIC ROSE. Revised and Enlarged by THEODORE BESTERMAN. 2 vols. £1 10*s. net.*
STUDIES OF SAVAGES AND SEX
Edited by THEODORE BESTERMAN.
10*s.* 6*d. net.*
DRESS, DRINKS AND DRUMS. Edited by THEODORE BESTERMAN. 12*s.* 6*d. net.*

DUGDALE (E. T. S.)
GERMAN DIPLOMATIC DOCUMENTS, 1871–1914
Selected from the Documents published by the German Foreign Office. In 4 vols. Vol. I, 1871–90. Vol. II, 1891–8. Vol. III, 1898–1910. Vol. IV, 1911–1914.
Each £1 1*s. net.*

EDWARDES (Tickner)
THE LORE OF THE HONEY-BEE
Illustrated. 7*s.* 6*d.* and 3*s.* 6*d. net.*
BEEKEEPING FOR ALL
Illustrated. 3*s.* 6*d. net.*
THE BEE-MASTER OF WARRILOW
Illustrated. 7*s.* 6*d. net.*
BEE-KEEPING DO'S AND DONT'S
2*s.* 6*d. net.*
LIFT-LUCK ON SOUTHERN ROADS
Illustrated. 5*s. net.*

EINSTEIN (Albert)
RELATIVITY : THE SPECIAL AND GENERAL THEORY 5*s. net.*
SIDELIGHTS ON RELATIVITY
3*s.* 6*d. net.*
THE MEANING OF RELATIVITY
5*s. net.*
THE BROWNIAN MOVEMENT
5*s. net.*

EISLER (Robert)
THE MESSIAH JESUS AND JOHN THE BAPTIST : according to Flavius Josephus' recently rediscovered 'Capture of Jerusalem' and the other Jewish and Christian sources. Translated by A. HAGGERTY KRAPPE.
Illustrated. *Demy* 8*vo.* £2 2*s. net.*

FIELD (G. C.)
MORAL THEORY 6*s. net.*
PLATO AND HIS CONTEMPORARIES
12*s.* 6*d. net.*

FYLEMAN (Rose)
FAIRIES AND CHIMNEYS
THE FAIRY GREEN
THE FAIRY FLUTE
THE RAINBOW CAT
EIGHT LITTLE PLAYS FOR CHILDREN
FORTY GOOD-NIGHT TALES
FAIRIES AND FRIENDS
THE ADVENTURE CLUB
FORTY GOOD-MORNING TALES
SEVEN LITTLE PLAYS FOR CHILDREN
TWENTY TEA-TIME TALES
Each 3*s.* 6*d. net.*

FYLEMAN (Rose)—*continued*
THE DOLLS' HOUSE
Illustrated by MARGARET TEMPEST. 5*s. net.*
GAY GO UP
Illustrated by DECIE MERWIN. 5*s. net.*
THE ROSE FYLEMAN FAIRY BOOK
Illustrated by HILDA MILLER. 10*s.* 6*d. net.*
A GARLAND OF ROSES: COLLECTED POEMS
Illustrated by RENÉ BULL. 8*s.* 6*d. net.*

GIBBON (Edward)
THE DECLINE AND FALL OF THE ROMAN EMPIRE
With Notes, Appendixes and Maps, by J. B. BURY. Illustrated. 7 vols. *Demy 8vo.* 15*s. net* each volume. Also, unillustrated. *Crown 8vo.* 7*s.* 6*d. net* each volume.

GLADSTONE (Mary) (Mrs. Drew)
HER DIARIES AND LETTERS
Illustrated. £1 1*s. net.*

GLOVER (T. R.)
VIRGIL
THE CONFLICT OF RELIGIONS IN THE EARLY ROMAN EMPIRE
POETS AND PURITANS
Each 10*s.* 6*d. net.*
FROM PERICLES TO PHILIP
12*s.* 6*d. net.*

GRAHAM (Harry)
THE WORLD WE LAUGH IN: More Deportmental Ditties
Illustrated by 'FISH'. *Eighth Edition.* 5*s. net.*
STRAINED RELATIONS
Illustrated by H. STUART MENZIES and HENDY. 6*s. net.*
THE WORLD'S WORKERS
Illustrated by 'FOUGASSE'. 5*s. net.*
ADAM'S APPLES
Illustrated by JOHN REYNOLDS. 5*s. net.*

GRAHAME (Kenneth)
THE WIND IN THE WILLOWS
207*th Thousand.* 7*s.* 6*d. net.*
Also illustrated by WYNDHAM PAYNE. 7*s.* 6*d. net.*
Also unillustrated.
Cloth, 3*s.* 6*d. net.*
Green Morocco, 7*s.* 6*d. net.*
See also **Milne (A. A.)**

HADFIELD (J. A.)
PSYCHOLOGY AND MORALS
Eighth Edition. Crown 8vo. 6*s. net.*

HALL (H. R.)
THE ANCIENT HISTORY OF THE NEAR EAST
Illustrated. £1 1*s. net.*
THE CIVILIZATION OF GREECE IN THE BRONZE AGE
Illustrated. £1 10*s. net.*
A SEASON'S WORK AT UR OF THE CHALDEES. Illustrated. £1 5*s. net.*

HEATON (Rose Henniker)
THE PERFECT HOSTESS
Decorated by A. E. TAYLOR.
7*s.* 6*d. net.* Gift Edition, £1 1*s. net.*

HERBERT (A. P.)
HONEYBUBBLE & CO. 6*s. net.*
MISLEADING CASES IN THE COMMON LAW. With an Introduction by LORD HEWART. 5*s. net.*
MORE MISLEADING CASES 5*s. net.*
WISDOM FOR THE WISE
Illustrated by GEORGE MORROW. 5*s. net.*
THE WHEREFORE AND THE WHY
Illustrated by GEORGE MORROW. 3*s.* 6*d. net.*
THE BOMBER GIPSY 3*s.* 6*d. net.*
THE SECRET BATTLE 3*s.* 6*d. net.*
TANTIVY TOWERS 2*s.* 6*d. net.*
MR. MAFFERTY 5*s. net.*

HOLDSWORTH (Sir W. S.)
A HISTORY OF ENGLISH LAW
Nine Volumes. £1 5*s. net each.*

HUDSON (W. H.)
A SHEPHERD'S LIFE
Illustrated. 10*s.* 6*d. net.*
Also unillustrated. 3*s.* 6*d. net.*

HUTTON (Edward)
CITIES OF SICILY
Illustrated. 10*s.* 6*d. net.*
MILAN AND LOMBARDY
THE CITIES OF ROMAGNA AND THE MARCHES
SIENA AND SOUTHERN TUSCANY
NAPLES AND SOUTHERN ITALY
Illustrated. *Each* 8*s.* 6*d. net.*
A WAYFARER IN UNKNOWN TUSCANY
THE CITIES OF SPAIN
THE CITIES OF UMBRIA
COUNTRY WALKS ABOUT FLORENCE
ROME
FLORENCE AND NORTHERN TUSCANY
VENICE AND VENETIA
Illustrated. *Each* 7*s.* 6*d. net.*

INGE (W. R.), D.D., Dean of St. Paul's
CHRISTIAN MYSTICISM
(The Bampton Lectures of 1899).
Sixth Edition. 7*s.* 6*d. net.*

KIPLING (Rudyard)
BARRACK-ROOM BALLADS
255th Thousand.
THE SEVEN SEAS
186th Thousand.
THE FIVE NATIONS
143rd Thousand.
DEPARTMENTAL DITTIES
117th Thousand.
THE YEARS BETWEEN
95th Thousand.
Four Editions of these famous volumes of poems are now published, viz. :—
Crown 8vo. Buckram, 7*s.* 6*d. net.*
Fcap. 8vo. Cloth, 6*s. net.*
Leather 7*s.* 6*d. net.*
Service Edition. Two volumes each book. *Square Fcap. 8vo.* 3*s. net* each volume.
A KIPLING ANTHOLOGY—VERSE
Sixth Edition.
Leather 7*s.* 6*d. net.*
Cloth 6*s. net* and 3*s.* 6*d. net.*
TWENTY POEMS FROM RUDYARD KIPLING
486th Thousand. 1*s. net.*
A CHOICE OF SONGS
Second Edition. 2*s. net.*

LAISTNER (M. L. W.)
THOUGHT AND LETTERS IN WESTERN EUROPE (A.D. 500–900). 15*s. net.*

LAMB (Charles and Mary)
THE COMPLETE WORKS
Edited by E. V. LUCAS. Six Volumes. With Frontispieces. 6*s. net each.*
SELECTED LETTERS
Edited by G. T. CLAPTON. 3*s.* 6*d. net.*
THE CHARLES LAMB DAY BOOK
Compiled by E. V. LUCAS. 6*s. net.*

LANKESTER (Sir Ray)
SCIENCE FROM AN EASY CHAIR
SCIENCE FROM AN EASY CHAIR : Second Series
DIVERSIONS OF A NATURALIST
GREAT AND SMALL THINGS
Illustrated. *Each* 7*s.* 6*d. net.*
SECRETS OF EARTH AND SEA
Illustrated. 8*s.* 6*d. net.*

LINDRUM (Walter)
BILLIARDS. Illustrated. 6*s. net.*

LODGE (Sir Oliver)
MAN AND THE UNIVERSE
7*s.* 6*d. net* and 3*s.* 6*d. net.*
THE SURVIVAL OF MAN
7*s.* 6*d. net.*
RAYMOND 10*s.* 6*d. net.*
RAYMOND REVISED 6*s. net.*
MODERN PROBLEMS 3*s.* 6*d. net.*
REASON AND BELIEF 3*s.* 6*d. net.*
THE SUBSTANCE OF FAITH
2*s. net.*
RELATIVITY 1*s. net.*
CONVICTION OF SURVIVAL 2*s. net.*

LUCAS (E. V.)
THE LIFE OF CHARLES LAMB
2 Vols. £1 1*s. net.*
THE COLVINS AND THEIR FRIENDS
£1 1*s. net.*
VERMEER THE MAGICAL 5*s. net.*
A WANDERER IN ROME
A WANDERER IN HOLLAND
A WANDERER IN LONDON
LONDON REVISITED (Revised)
A WANDERER IN PARIS
A WANDERER IN FLORENCE
A WANDERER IN VENICE
Each 10*s.* 6*d. net.*
A WANDERER AMONG PICTURES
8*s.* 6*d. net.*
E. V. LUCAS'S LONDON £1 *net.*
INTRODUCING LONDON
INTRODUCING PARIS
Each 2*s.* 6*d. net.*
THE OPEN ROAD 6*s. net.*
Also, illustrated by CLAUDE A. SHEPPERSON, A.R.W.S.
10*s.* 6*d. net.*
Also, India Paper.
Leather, 7*s.* 6*d. net.*
THE JOY OF LIFE
6*s. net. Leather Edition,* 7*s.* 6*d. net.*
Also, India Paper.
Leather, 7*s.* 6*d. net.*
THE GENTLEST ART 3*s.* 6*d. net.*
And THE SECOND POST 3*s.* 6*d. net.*
Also together in one volume.
7*s.* 6*d. net.*
FIRESIDE AND SUNSHINE
CHARACTER AND COMEDY
GOOD COMPANY
ONE DAY AND ANOTHER
OLD LAMPS FOR NEW
LOITERER'S HARVEST
LUCK OF THE YEAR
EVENTS AND EMBROIDERIES
A FRONDED ISLE
A ROVER I WOULD BE
GIVING AND RECEIVING
HER INFINITE VARIETY
ENCOUNTERS AND DIVERSIONS
TURNING THINGS OVER
Each 3*s.* 6*d. net.*

LUCAS (E. V.)—*continued*
CLOUD AND SILVER
A BOSWELL OF BAGHDAD
'TWIXT EAGLE AND DOVE
THE PHANTOM JOURNAL
ZIGZAGS IN FRANCE
TRAVELLER'S LUCK
VISIBILITY GOOD *Each* 6*s. net.*
FRENCH LEAVES
Illustrated. 5*s. net.*
ROVING EAST AND ROVING WEST
5*s. net.*
Mr. Punch's COUNTY SONGS
Illustrated by E. H. SHEPARD.
10*s.* 6*d. net.*
'THE MORE I SEE OF MEN . . .'
OUT OF A CLEAR SKY
IF DOGS COULD WRITE
'. . . AND SUCH SMALL DEER'
Each 3*s.* 6*d. net.*
THE PEKINESE NATIONAL ANTHEM
Illustrated by PERSIS KIRMSE.
1*s. net.*
See also **Lamb (Charles).**

LYND (Robert)
IT'S A FINE WORLD 5*s. net.*
THE GREEN MAN
THE PLEASURES OF IGNORANCE
THE GOLDFISH
THE LITTLE ANGEL
THE BLUE LION
THE PEAL OF BELLS
THE MONEY-BOX
THE ORANGE TREE *Each* 3*s.* 6*d. net.*

McDOUGALL (William)
AN INTRODUCTION TO SOCIAL PSYCHOLOGY 10*s.* 6*d. net.*
NATIONAL WELFARE AND NATIONAL DECAY 6*s. net.*
AN OUTLINE OF PSYCHOLOGY
10*s.* 6*d. net.*
AN OUTLINE OF ABNORMAL PSYCHOLOGY 15*s. net.*
BODY AND MIND 12*s.* 6*d. net.*
CHARACTER AND THE CONDUCT OF LIFE 10*s.* 6*d. net.*
MODERN MATERIALISM AND EMERGENT EVOLUTION 7*s.* 6*d. net.*
ETHICS AND SOME MODERN WORLD PROBLEMS 7*s.* 6*d. net.*
A BRIEF OUTLINE OF PSYCHOLOGY: Normal and Abnormal
8*s.* 6*d. net.*

MALLET (Sir C. E.)
A HISTORY OF THE UNIVERSITY OF OXFORD
In 3 vols. *Each* £1 1*s. net.*

MAETERLINCK (Maurice)
THE BLUE BIRD 6*s. net.*
Also, illustrated by F. CAYLEY ROBINSON. 10*s.* 6*d. net.*
OUR ETERNITY 6*s. net.*
THE UNKNOWN GUEST 6*s. net.*
POEMS 5*s. net.*
THE WRACK OF THE STORM
6*s. net.*
THE BURGOMASTER OF STILEMONDE
5*s. net.*
THE BETROTHAL 6*s. net.*
MOUNTAIN PATHS 6*s. net.*
THE GREAT SECRET 7*s.* 6*d. net.*
THE CLOUD THAT LIFTED and THE POWER OF THE DEAD 7*s.* 6*d. net.*
MARY MAGDALENE 2*s. net.*

MARLOWE (Christopher)
THE WORKS. In 6 volumes.
General Editor, R. H. CASE.
THE LIFE OF MARLOWE, by C. F. TUCKER BROOKE, and DIDO. Edited by the Same. 8*s.* 6*d. net.*
TAMBURLAINE, I AND II. Edited by U. M. ELLIS-FERMOR. 10*s.* 6*d. net.*
THE JEW OF MALTA and THE MASSACRE AT PARIS
Edited by H. S. BENNETT.
10*s.* 6*d. net.*
POEMS
Edited by L. C. MARTIN.
10*s.* 6*d net.*

MASEFIELD (John)
ON THE SPANISH MAIN 8*s.* 6*d. net.*
A SAILOR'S GARLAND 3*s.* 6*d. net.*
SEA LIFE IN NELSON'S TIME
7*s.* 6*d. net.*

METHUEN (Sir A.)
AN ANTHOLOGY OF MODERN VERSE
232*nd Thousand.*
SHAKESPEARE TO HARDY: An Anthology of English Lyrics
28*th Thousand.*
Each, Cloth, 6*s. net.*
Leather, 7*s.* 6*d. net.*

MILNE (A. A.)
BY WAY OF INTRODUCTION 6*s. net.*
TOAD OF TOAD HALL
A Play founded on Kenneth Grahame's 'The Wind in the Willows.' 5*s. net.*
THOSE WERE THE DAYS: Collected Stories 7*s.* 6*d. net.*
NOT THAT IT MATTERS
IF I MAY
THE SUNNY SIDE
THE RED HOUSE MYSTERY
ONCE A WEEK
THE HOLIDAY ROUND

MILNE (A. A.)—*continued*
THE DAY'S PLAY
MR. PIM PASSES BY
Each 3*s*. 6*d*. *net*.
WHEN WE WERE VERY YOUNG
211*th Thousand*.
WINNIE-THE-POOH
118*th Thousand*.
NOW WE ARE SIX
119*th Thousand*.
THE HOUSE AT POOH CORNER
105*th Thousand*.
Each illustrated by E. H. SHEPARD.
7*s*. 6*d*. *net*. *Leather*, 10*s*. 6*d* *net*.
THE CHRISTOPHER ROBIN STORY BOOK. *Third Edition*.
Illustrated by E. H. SHEPARD.
5*s*. *net*.
THE CHRISTOPHER ROBIN BIRTH-DAY BOOK
Illustrated by E. H. SHEPARD.
3*s*. 6*d*. *net*.

MILNE (A. A.) and FRASER-SIMSON (H.)
FOURTEEN SONGS FROM 'WHEN WE WERE VERY YOUNG'
Thirteenth Edition. 7*s*. 6*d*. *net*.
TEDDY BEAR AND OTHER SONGS FROM 'WHEN WE WERE VERY YOUNG' 7*s*. 6*d*. *net*.
THE KING'S BREAKFAST
Third Edition. 3*s*. 6*d*. *net*.
SONGS FROM 'NOW WE ARE SIX'
Second Edition. 7*s*. 6*d*. *net*.
MORE 'VERY YOUNG' SONGS
7*s*. 6*d*. *net*.
THE HUMS OF POOH 7*s*. 6*d*. *net*.
Words by A. A. MILNE.
Music by H. FRASER-SIMSON.
Decorations by E. H. SHEPARD.

MORTON (H. V.)
THE HEART OF LONDON
35*th Thousand*. 3*s*. 6*d*. *net*.
Also with Scissor Cuts by L. HUMMEL. 6*s*. *net*.
THE SPELL OF LONDON
25*th Thousand*.
THE NIGHTS OF LONDON
18*th Thousand*. *Each* 3*s*. 6*d*. *net*.
IN SEARCH OF ENGLAND
74*th Thousand*.
THE CALL OF ENGLAND
35*th Thousand*.
IN SEARCH OF SCOTLAND
96*th Thousand*.
IN SEARCH OF IRELAND
40*th Thousand*.
IN SEARCH OF WALES
Each illustrated. 7*s*. 6*d*. *net*.

NEUBURGER (Albert)
THE TECHNICAL ARTS AND SCIENCES OF THE ANCIENTS
Translated by H. L. BROSE.
Illustrated. £2 2*s*. *net*.

OMAN (Sir Charles)
A HISTORY OF THE ART OF WAR IN THE MIDDLE AGES, A.D. 378–1485
2 vols. Illustrated. £1 16*s*. *net*.
STUDIES IN THE NAPOLEONIC WARS
8*s*. 6*d*. *net*.

PERRY (W. J.)
THE ORIGIN OF MAGIC AND RELIGION
THE GROWTH OF CIVILIZATION
Each 6*s*. *net*.
THE CHILDREN OF THE SUN
£1 1*s*. *net*.

PETRIE (Sir Flinders)
A HISTORY OF EGYPT
In 6 Volumes.
Vol. I. FROM THE IST TO THE XVITH DYNASTY
Eleventh Edition, Revised.
12*s*. *net*.
Vol. II. THE XVIITH AND XVIIITH DYNASTIES
Seventh Edition, Revised. 9*s*. *net*.
Vol. III. XIXTH TO XXXTH DYNASTIES
Third Edition. 12*s*. *net*.
Vol. IV. EGYPT UNDER THE PTOLEMAIC DYNASTY
By EDWYN BEVAN. 15*s*. *net*.
Vol. V. EGYPT UNDER ROMAN RULE
By J. G. MILNE.
Third Edition, Revised. 12*s*. *net*.
Vol. VI. EGYPT IN THE MIDDLE AGES
By STANLEY LANE POOLE.
Fourth Edition. 10*s*. *net*.

PONSONBY OF SHULBREDE (Lord)
ENGLISH DIARIES £1 1*s*. *net*.
MORE ENGLISH DIARIES
12*s*. 6*d*. *net*.
SCOTTISH AND IRISH DIARIES
10*s*. 6*d*. *net*.

RUTTER (Frank)
EL GRECO. Illustrated. £1 16*s*. *net*.

SELLAR (W. C.) and YEATMAN (R. J.)
1066 AND ALL THAT
Illustrated by JOHN REYNOLDS.
63*rd Thousand*. 5*s*. *net*.

STEVENSON (R. L.)
THE LETTERS Edited by Sir SIDNEY COLVIN. 4 Vols. *Each* 6s. *net.*

STOW (G. W.) and BLEEK (Dorothea F.)
ROCK PAINTINGS IN SOUTH AFRICA
Illustrated. £2 2s. *net.*

SURTEES (R. S.)
HANDLEY CROSS
MR. SPONGE'S SPORTING TOUR
ASK MAMMA
MR. FACEY ROMFORD'S HOUNDS
PLAIN OR RINGLETS?
HILLINGDON HALL
Each illustrated. 7s. 6*d. net.*
JORROCKS'S JAUNTS AND JOLLITIES
HAWBUCK GRANGE
Each illustrated. 6s. *net.*

TAYLOR (A. E.)
PLATO: THE MAN AND HIS WORK
£1 1s. *net.*
PLATO: TIMÆUS AND CRITIAS
6s. *net.*
ELEMENTS OF METAPHYSICS
12s. 6*d. net.*

TILDEN (William T.)
THE ART OF LAWN TENNIS
Revised Edition.
SINGLES AND DOUBLES
Each illustrated. 6s. *net.*
THE COMMON SENSE OF LAWN TENNIS
MATCH PLAY AND THE SPIN OF THE BALL
Each illustrated. 5s. *net.*

TILESTON (Mary W.)
DAILY STRENGTH FOR DAILY NEEDS
Thirty-fourth Edition. 3s. 6*d. net.*
India Paper. *Leather*, 6s. *net.*

TRAPP (Oswald Graf)
THE ARMOURY OF THE CASTLE OF CHURBURG
Translated by J. G. MANN.
Richly illustrated.
Limited to 400 copies.
£4 14s. 6*d. net.*

UNDERHILL (Evelyn)
MYSTICISM. *Revised Edition.* 15s. *net.*
THE LIFE OF THE SPIRIT AND THE LIFE OF TO-DAY 7s. 6*d. net.*
MAN AND THE SUPERNATURAL
7s. 6*d. net.*
THE GOLDEN SEQUENCE 7s. 6*d. net.*
CONCERNING THE INNER LIFE
2s. *net.*
THE HOUSE OF THE SOUL 2s. *net.*

VARDON (Harry)
HOW TO PLAY GOLF
Illustrated. *Nineteenth Edition.*
5s. *net.*

WELD-BLUNDELL (Dom B.)
SELF-DISCIPLINE AND HOLINESS
5s. *net.*

WILDE (Oscar)
THE WORKS
In 16 Vols. *Each* 6s. 6*d. net.*
I. LORD ARTHUR SAVILE'S CRIME AND THE PORTRAIT OF MR. W. H.
II. THE DUCHESS OF PADUA
III. POEMS
IV. LADY WINDERMERE'S FAN
V. A WOMAN OF NO IMPORTANCE
VI. AN IDEAL HUSBAND
VII. THE IMPORTANCE OF BEING EARNEST
VIII. A HOUSE OF POMEGRANATES
IX. INTENTIONS
X. DE PROFUNDIS AND PRISON LETTERS
XI. ESSAYS
XII. SALOME, A FLORENTINE TRAGEDY, and LA SAINTE COURTISANE
XIV. SELECTED PROSE OF OSCAR WILDE
XV. ART AND DECORATION
XVI. FOR LOVE OF THE KING
5s. *net.*
XVII. VERA, OR THE NIHILISTS

WILLIAMSON (G. C.)
THE BOOK OF FAMILLE ROSE
Richly Illustrated. £8 8s. *net.*